Modern Masters

A Personal pantheon

Music
Painting
Television
Literature

- Dhiraj Singh

For my brothers

We are half a dozen

Table of Contents

Television

Literature

Jimi Hendrix: Voodoo Child in a Room Full of Mirrors

'Will the wind ever remember
The names it has blown in the past
And with his crutch, it's old age,
and it's wisdom
It whispers no, this will be the last
And the wind cries Mary'
-'The Wind Cries Mary' from the album 'Are You Experienced'

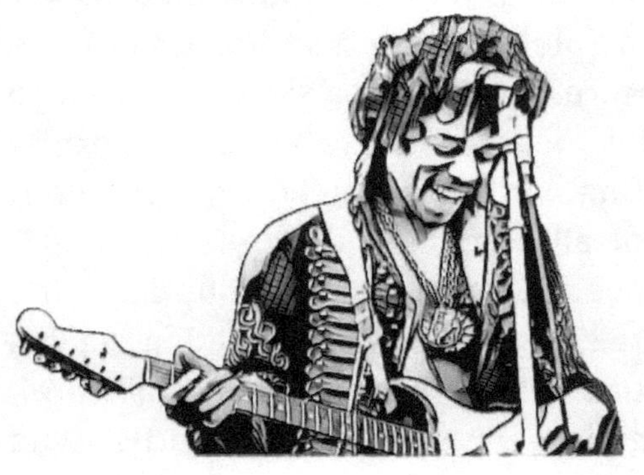

In the first album of 'Jimi Hendrix Experience'- a band built around the emerging phenomenon called, well, Jimi Hendrix, Jimi shouts 'manic depression is a frustrating mess' in the microphone, then picks up his guitar and shows us the howling twisted abyss of the torment. Not for nothing, often he is rated as the greatest guitarist of all time. With a dizzying level of glossy showmanship daring chutzpah, it is easy to be suspicious of the label of genius. However, in Hendrix, we are dealing with the real thing. His voice (as well as sounds) were original and he created a repertoire that has strands which still define popular culture. He is revered by the psychedelic scene, his folksy songs have a status of a benchmark (remember 'Little Wing'), his blues have given rise to a veritable industry of cover versions (please hear 'Voodoo Child'). He was unsure of his singing skills but listen to any of his songs and sense his vocal dexterity competing with extremely expert guitar. Shorn of all psychedelic haze, stage antics and above all untimely mysterious death (he died at 27 supposedly suffocating on his vomit under the influence of barbiturate), Jimi Hendrix was a truly gifted artist who could realize astonishing successes in a short span of four years when he achieved stardom.

Jimi Hendrix forms part of the tragic troika of 'Js'- Jim Morrison, Janis Joplin and Jimmy Hendrix. All three created something that has endured and more or less epitomized the music of their time. However the tragic shortness of their creative journey (Janis died 13 days after Jimi and Jim died less than six months later all of them were 27) is also indicative of the uneasy relationship between direction of their creativity and a life sustaining way of living. Some of the fellow travellers survived (Rolling Stone, members of Beatles sans Lennon, Clapton, Dylan come to mind among others). Despite the short time period when three Js acquired centre-stage, their legacy survives and many tributaries of popular western music continue to echo their throbbing intensity and improvisational guts.

Jimmy (James Marshall Hendrix) was born in Seattle on November 27th, 1942. His father was serving in the army and got to see his son quite late and is responsible for 'James' in the name as mother Lucille, originally named him 'Johnny Allen Hendrix'. Hendrix got his first guitar at the age of almost sixteen (remember he was dead at twenty seven). A self taught guitarist, Jimi Hendrix was shaped by the forces of blues like B B King and Muddy Water. In fact, he played behind quite a few of them such as Sam

Cooke, Little Richard, Wilson Pickett, Jackie Wilson, Ike-Tina Turner, and B.B. King. As a club musician in New York, he was part of a varied lot like the Isley Brothers, King Curtis, John Paul Hammond, and Curtis Knight. Earlier, he played in high school bands before enlisting in the U.S. Army in 1959 only to be discharged on medical grounds in 1961.

In 1965 Hendrix formed his own band, 'Jimmy James and the Blue Flames,' to play at Greenwich Village coffeehouses. He was noticed by Chas Chandler of the Animals who took him to London, capital of cool at that time, in 1966. London was the proverbial turning point. Within a week of landing there he jammed with Eric Clapton, created a stir for his new sounds and soon had his most productive partners in Noel Redding on bass and Mitch Mitchell on drums. 'Jimi Hendrix Experience' was born. Hendrix literally lit up the London music scene with his edgy rock performances. His blues that were theoretically placed in the definitional parameters of the genre, rebelled silently just at the most game-changing points. Generous English pantheon (Beatles, Clapton, Pete Townshend to count a few) not only accepted him but turned into ardent fans. Townshend was to write later "It was a high form of eroticism, almost spiritual in quality. There was a sense of wanting to possess him (Hendrix) and wanting to be a part of him, to know how he did what he did because he was so powerfully affecting. Johnny Rotten did it, Kurt Cobain did it...... he had a kind of alchemist's ability; when he was on the stage, he changed."

His return to the US in 1967 is part of folklore. A neglected side artist of yore came to rapturous applause in Monterey Pop Festival in 1967 (Sitar maestro Ravi Shankar was another artist introduced to the West by the festival). America was charmed, an overwhelmed 24 year old Jimi set his guitar on fire as a gesture of gratitude, "I'm gonna sacrifice something here I really love. Don't think I'm silly doin' this, because I don't think I'm losin' my mind .... But today, I think it's the right thing .... There's nothing more I can do than this" he is believed to have said. He was dead within three years of Monterey. It is difficult to believe that he was famous and alive for less than four years and cut only three proper albums officially. His shadow looms very large and virtually every note he struck has been commercially exploited.

His early singles "Hey Joe," "Purple Haze" and "Burning of the Midnight Lamp" flowered into one of the most influential albums of all time 'Are You Experienced?' The music of the late sixties has an appeal and the era evokes nostalgia. Sometimes the smell of self-destructive creativity masks the incredible beauty of the musical output of the period. 'Are You Experienced?' has the force and even naked destruction to showcase the nihilistic brutality of the period but above all it is an anthem of creativity, vitality expanded genius that flourishes at a particular epoch of history without any rational explanation. Want to experience the sixties without feeling smug about advancement in music and narration-'Are You Experienced?' can be a revealing as well as humbling experience.

His next album —'Axis: Bold As Love' was low on sonic flourishes but nevertheless equally adventurous in scope and intended impact. 'Little Wing' is one of the most loved songs in the formidable Jimi repertoire. Fiery 'Crosstown Traffic,' 'Voodoo Child (Slight

Return)' soulful 'Rainy Day, Dream Away,' '1983...(A Merman I Should Turn to Be),' 'Moon, Turn the Tides...gently gently away' yes you get the picture of consolidation of a hyper ambition. The third album 'Electric Ladyland' was most completely his work as he had better creative control due to changed circumstances.

Hendrix was a technical virtuoso who could understand and exploit the hidden potential of musical gizmos and create new sound in a most hauntingly sustainable way. If the studio liberated him to conjure an uncontrollable sonic universe, stage was his natural home- he was a performer of hypnotic magnetism. His cool was totally his own and survives in the enduring rock iconography. He was a 'Voodoo Child' capable of creating an unimaginably alluring atmosphere with his stage athleticism, antics that bordered on bizarre and tricks that endeared him to the crowd. The sexual overtones were heightened by his mannerism and lyrical eroticism of his music. His death contributed to his mystique. A lesser artist would have been swamped by the hoopla but his music survives. He said he wanted to be taken seriously as a musician and did not want to clown any more. 'Genius of doubt', a phrase used for artist Cezanne, is aptly applicable to him. Jimi's articulation, both verbal and musical, was tentative in appearance as if something unruly had been let out without a proper plan. Rough texture and unfinished feel added to the wild confusion. However, the end product is almost always unalloyed beauty. In fact the hint of slight anarchy is integral to many interesting pieces of modern creativity but very few had the wherewithal to goad the torrential chaos into enduring beauty as Jimi Hendrix has done. Protean persona of the genius continues to define cool, making it hard to believe he is dead for almost six decades.

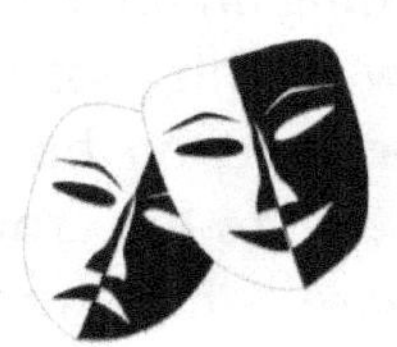

Weird Scenes Inside the Goldmine - Death Lust of Jim Morrison

"This is the end, beautiful friend.
It hurts to set you free,
But you'll never follow me.
The end of laughter and soft lies.
The end of nights we tried to die.
This is the... end."
-From The End by The Doors

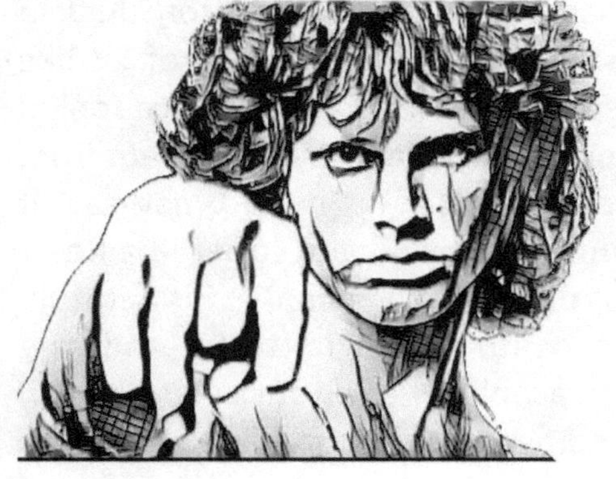

Jim Morrison shares his final resting place with the likes of Chopin, Oscar Wilde and hundreds of poets, aristocrats and geniuses. However, only his grave in Père-Lachaise cemetery in Paris is watched over by a round the clock cop as it is not only the busiest site of this extraordinary place but generates a different type of hysteria that would have amused Oscar Wilde into one of his most caustic witticisms.

Morrison wanted to be known as a poet and had a flair for words. He saw himself as a poet trapped in a Rock star's body. His band, mythical 'The Doors' faced the classical paradox of the day - gains from the allure of a dangerous persona and downfall brought by the same. A ravaged Morrison died in Paris on July 3, 1971 at the age of 27 like other two 'Js' Jimi Hendrix and Janice Joplin. Whatever nostalgic fans (most of them from the generation after his death) may say, it was a diminished icon who suffered a heart attack (as per official version) in his bathtub. However, death is integral to his enduring legend- a cacophony of mysticism, sexuality, poetry and psychedelic haze. "He's hot, he's sexy and he's dead" shouted the cover of Rolling Stone Magazine ten years after Morrison's death. It was correct then, it is true now.

Later half of the sixties was a good time for Morrison to be alive. The raging counterculture with its angst ridden yearnings, primal sexuality, unhinged drunkenness and a wildly seductive notion of enlightenment- was ready for him. He came and lent a veneer of sheer sexiness to the excesses of his era. Continued popularity of the music of the period owes a great deal to the hankering for the nostalgia for a richly complex experience imbued with rage, lust, spirituality, freedom and an unapologetic flirtation with death and destruction. It was youth's way of gaining access to unimagined possibilities- a vision of hope and deadly charms of anarchy.

Morrison remains a key figure on the cultural landscape of the century gone by and still looms large. James Douglas "Jim" Morrison was born in the family of a ranking navy officer on December 8, 1943. He met Ray Menzarek, a classically trained pianist, while doing a Film course at UCLA Graduate School of Film. Morrison's poetic potential was evident to Manzarek and they decided to collaborate. Manzarek met John Densmore, who brought in Robby Krieger. The band's christening was done by Morrison. 'The Doors' came from William Blake through Aldous Huxley's book on mescaline, The

Doors of Perception. Blake had written and Huxley had quoted "If the doors of perception were cleansed everything would appear to man as it is, infinite." That was 1965 and in 1966 they were fired from Whisky-a-Go-Go club where they were the house band, for oedipal explicitness of 'The End'. Thus began the firming up of the 'Lizard King' persona of Morrison. In a poem that appeared on the sleeves of their album "Waiting For The Sun" Morrison pronounced "I am the Lizard King, I can do anything." The moniker stuck. The band is credited with hot albums like The Doors, Strange Days, Waiting for the Sun, The Soft Parade, Morrison Hotel and L A Woman.

Morrison's aura of unpredictability and dark potential gained in strength very quickly. His 'inspired exhibitionism' made sure that 'whatever he did was seen as brilliant or brilliantly calculated'. In December 1967 he was arrested for public obscenity at a concert in New Haven, and in August 1968 he was arrested for disorderly conduct aboard an airplane enroute to Phoenix. All that added to the dangerous appeal of his poisonous charms. But he was riding a tiger and he was slipping. His March 1969 arrest in Miami for exhibiting "lewd and lascivious behavior by exposing his private parts" finally managed to dent Morrison's sense of invincibility. The singer was restricted to Miami for the good part of the year for the court proceedings. The charges were never proved but the tension brought home the realization of harsh realities. It affected concert schedules and many performances were cancelled.

Soon after L.A. Woman was recorded in 1971, Morrison informed the group that he was leaving. A depleted Morrison both physically and emotionally moved to Paris. He was accompanied by his long-time companion Pamela Courson. In his estate controversy later, Courson was legally treated as his wife. Jim also had a Celtic wedding with Patricia Kennealy which was never recognized by law. Morrison led a quiet life in Paris and tried to write poems. Days of raunchy taboo-bending were over.

As per official version, he died of heart failure in his bathtub in 1971 at age 27. His death gained a mysterious aura partly because news of his death was not made public until days after his burial in Paris'

Père-Lachaise cemetery. Many conspiracy theories were floating. Many fans still refuse to believe Morrison is dead. Sam Bernett, former manager of the Rock 'n' Roll Circus nightclub of Paris, claimed in his book that instead of dying of a heart attack in a bathtub Morrison overdosed on heroin on a toilet seat in the club. He claimed that he was dissuaded by Morrison's drug dealers from calling the police. He and some other people brought the body to the apartment Morrison had rented, and staged his body in the bathtub. Whatever the circumstances, the death was in accordance with the tradition of high-profile demises-contentious, mysterious and above all sudden. Courson, one of the few people who saw Morrison's corpse, died in Hollywood of a heroin overdose on April 25, 1974, she too was 27.

If Jimi Hendrix was raw talent, Jim was structured for fame with that elusive characteristic that lures without any obvious reason. His appeal was much more natural or, more accurately, animal. Hendrix was a master of improvisational panache, Morrison's voice has been referred to as a "beautiful pond for anything to drown in."

While Hendrix was 'vodoo child' Jim was 'Satan's Seraph' who epitomized sexual nirvana with his hint of spirituality, moody burst of creativity and difficult to contain rebellious streak. Creator of memorable lines, Hendrix was pathologically inarticulate while Jim was able to give intellectual crust to his views with great communicability. Though he was the main poetic force of the Doors, all the songs are attributed to the band. His interviews and one-liners stand testimony to his deliciously absurd poetic sensibilities. His poems did not find many takers among critics but they have a charm of their own. His devastating antics and relentless chase of chaos could not obscure his avant-garde sensibilities. Unlike many of his lyrics, Morrison was capable of unexpected tenderness in his poetry.

"She looked so sad in sleep
Like a friendly hand
just out of reach
A candle stranded on
a beach"

Contrast it with the absurd beauty of these lines from 'Rider on the Storm'
"There's a killer on the road

One is captivated by hints of other realms of consciousness when The Doors sing 'Swim to the moon' and 'penetrate the evening that the city sleeps to hide'. They are at their drunken best with 'L A Women', sex drips through 'Come on Baby Light My Fire' 'Roadhouse Blues' can set the tone for any rock party. 'The End' is a poetry of oedipal jolts, an odyssey that seeks to shock with casual profanity. 'Break on Through (to the Other Side)' is one of the anthems of rock. An absolute favourite is 'Riders on the Storm'. In the song, the silken barbarism of that sexy beast Morrison's voice gains its full grandeur along with the searing poetry of the absurd. Metallic texture of the shivery tones, throbbing keyboards of Ray Menzarek, the fluid lyrical guitar of Robby Krieger and the supple drums of John Dansmore make the sultry, languid and soothing experience of the song which is also full of violence and alienation. Sublime music masks the edginess which encapsulates the tortured zeitgeist of an epoch. Remove the hoopla created by wild antics of Morrison's flirtations with chaos, you get some really solid music. Howsoever romantic this flirtation may sound but lingering regret remains- a regret of losing out on many more such gems as mentioned above.

When Oliver Stone's eponymous movie on The Doors came in 1991, it was not subject to normal cinematic scrutiny deploying usual parameters of reviewing a movie. The movie was viewed and castigated through the lens of nostalgia. Learned critics were 'wincing at infidelities like absence of hope and light'. They saw in its failure a 'grim reminder of that we (Americans) have lost our pioneering cultural influence'. The New Yorker lamented the 'mean spiritedness that kept breaking through' the movie- the 'bad faith' and 'tabloid like sensibility'. Time Magazine was no less caustic, Richard Corliss wrote "Kilmer (Val Kilmer played Morrison) is just conventionally good-looking; he can't prowl like Blake's Tyger or pose with the sultry arrogance of a Beat poet. Nor does he have the intellectual seductiveness that made Morrison a toy of the hip literati. In short,

Kilmer is not Jim, and his casting denies The Doors the chance to be a meditation on the lure of sexual power." Yes you get the idea, sixties counterculture evokes extreme responses and rock was a religion with those who lived through the period and icons like Morrison, Hendrix and Joplin were its presiding deities.

Full Tilt Boogie: Kozmic Blues of Janis Joplin

"All caught up in a landslide,
bad luck pressing in from all sides
Got bucked off of my easy ride
buried alive in the blues."
-'Buried Alive' from the posthumous Janis Joplin Album 'Pearl'- She could not complete the vocals

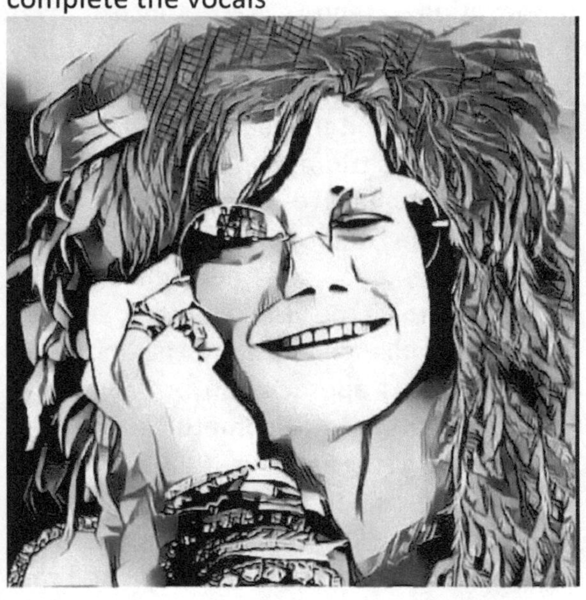

Compared to cocky insouciance of Jim Morrison and voodoo haze of Jimi Hendrix, Janis Joplin's insecurities about her background, talent and looks were there for all to see. Ironically, she was the most rugged stage performer of them all. Jimi and Jim were stage athletes but none of them went after the audience the way Janis did. Her larynx wrenching vocal antics, violent stomping and ubiquitous bottle of Southern Comfort created a tough Blues-mama shell around her. However, her need for appreciation and acceptance was transparent to all. Footage of the Monterey Pop Festival (which also marked the introduction of Sitar Maestro Ravi Shankar to the West and triumphant home coming of Jimi Hendrix) bears testimony to this naked need. At the end of the epoch-making performance, we see her milking the applause with all too visible hunger. One can sense her radiance grow by the moment. Everyone loves appreciation but for her it was affirmation of something deeper. "When I go on stage to sing, it's like the 'rush' that people experience when they take heavy dope. I talk to the audience, look into their eyes. I need them and they need me.

Sex is the closest I can come to explaining it, but it's more than sex. I get stoned from happiness. I want to do it until it isn't there anymore" She said in 1968. Very soon there wasn't any more of it. She died alone in a cheap Hollywood Motel of heroin overdose on October 4, 1970 and was discovered hours after her death. She died within three weeks of Jimi Hendrix's death, like him and Morrison later she too was 27.

Rolling Stone Magazine calls her "perhaps the premier blues-influenced rock singer of the late Sixties, and certainly one of the biggest female rock stars of her time." She remains a towering presence through her lasting legacy. Her redefinition of Blues and her unique rendition of average songs in her booze and dope ravaged voice are pioneering influences on musical firmament that was developing during her time. Fact of her being a prima donna of rock cannot be taken lightly. She was the most visible female singer to front a major band. She endures not just as a singer but as an archetype of longing and ambition. Her exalted iconography was sealed in that cheap motel room. Well-timed Photographs by Jim Marshall and strategic video footage added to her aura. She is frozen in public memory as those photographs of free spirit with hovering vulnerability. She looked like that very rarely but these photographs continue to portray the core of the phenomenon that Janis Joplin was – energy, ambition, longing and above all nihilistic lust for death. "People seem to have a high sense of drama about me. Maybe they can enjoy my music more if they think I'm destroying myself" She was quoted in her obituary in Time magazine.

Many of her self-doubts may have their origin in her growing up years in the sleepy town of Port Arthur in Texas. It is a refinery town where her father worked. A loner and misfit by the time she entered teens, Janis developed a taste for poetry and painting. She was attracted to blues and folk music. She was to become 'first hippie' of the town which was a result of bewilderment on her being rejected as outcast and a rebel. The town and the peers found it difficult to come to terms with her bizarre world view. She often described herself as a 'weirdo among fools'. She escaped to the West Coast when she was 17. Thus began a period of drifting with pot, booze and music.

San Francisco was the perfect place for her gypsy soul. She was at pains to explain that she was a beatnik not a hippie. Hippies believe the world could be a better place. "Beatniks believe things aren't going to get better and say the hell with it, stay stoned and have a good time", she propounded. Her links with home were never broken. Her letters to her parents and younger brother and sister reflect a caring person who wanted to remain a part of a nurturing whole. Her pleas to her parents regarding not giving up on her and her intention of continuing her education and advice to her sister portray a surprisingly 'normal' Janis yearning for simple order and care of a household- a far cry from a stomping yelling rock diva.

By the middle of 1966, Janis was called by old San Francisco friends who had cobbled together a promising rock band called Big Brother and the Holding Company. They adjusted well to each other. After initial tuning in, the Monterey Pop festival happened. She, the quintessential vagabond, hooked the appreciative crowd with her 'formless blues' belted out in shrieking, rasping and energetic style. The motley group of experimenting youngsters got Bob Dylan's manager Albert Grossman. Grossman proved an important enabler for the charged expansion of Janis Joplin myth. Their first record 'Cheap Thrills' went Gold in 1968. The Album had 'Piece of My Heart' which made the critics say that Janis does not use blues conventions to transcend the pain but to 'scream it out of existence'. ' Ball and Chain' and 'Turtle Blues' from the album further cemented her reputation as a singer to reckon with. Uniqueness of her voice and hysterical grandiosity of her performance is captured best in a piece about her in Vogue magazine in May 1968 "Janis assaults a song with her eyes, her hips, and her hair. She defies the key. shrieking over one line, sputtering over the next, and clutching the knees of a final stanza, begging it not to leave. When it does leave anyway, she stands like an assertive young tree, smiling breathlessly at the audience, which has just exploded. Janis Joplin can sing the chic off any listener."

Janis Joplin overgrew her band within a year. Big Brother and the Holding Company came unglued and Grossman who could visualise a glorious future for Joplin allowed the process of disintegration go unhindered. Joplin came out, taking only guitarist Sam Andrew with her to form the Kozmic Blues Band. The new band enjoyed commercial success but it could not recreate the creative garage band type of ambience of Big Brother. Joplin, one of the highest paid stars of her time, was without a band. Her last and most realized (though unfinished) Album 'Pearl' was with her new Full Tilt Boogie Band.

She became fairly regular on TV shows of that time. Her appearances on shows anchored by Dick Cavett, Tom Jones, and Ed Sullivan still remain the fodder for enumerable biographies and documentaries. TV appearances are another part of her fascinating iconography. Her views on her childhood, music and stage antics come most clearly in these shows and many of the insecurities were also addressed squarely in these shows. She appeared on the cover page of almost all major magazines like Time, Newsweek and Rolling stone. Newsweek's cover story was on 'Return of Blues' and they found Janis to represent the trend in May 1969. In 1988, Time magazine came out with an issue on '1968- Year That Shaped a Generation' and Janis was there alongside Vietnam and Robert Kennedy. This was an indication that she was a representative figure of the phenomenon of Rock. She told Time "We're not dispassionate professionals. We're passionate and sloppy. I'm an untutored native folk talent- I like that phrase, it's so pretentious." Generations have responded to this earthy charm of a mercurial talent in sync with the desperation and anarchy of her time.

Ironically, this desperation and loneliness was on wane when her turbulent life was cut short by the heroin overdose. Recording of Pearl was going very successfully. Producer Paul A. Rothchild was a dependable name and he ensured that some serious discipline and hard work went into the project. Janis was involved and enjoying the experience. She claimed to have kicked the drug habit. On a personal front she found love and was going steady with Seth Morgan. Paul Rothchild said later "During the sessions, I had never seen her happier. She was at the top of her form, having a great time. She said over and over again that this was the most fun she had ever had in a recording studio. Before, recording had always meant a lot of tension and fighting." This seeming revival makes the sense of loss even greater.

Unfulfilled potential remains a lingering pain in such untimely demises. However, the appeal of such lives is, in fact, rooted in the abruptness of their end. Myth building is a complex process and it certainly appears that sense of loss and aura of death take a place of pride in this dynamics. Who knows how Jimi Hendrix would have looked and felt like at 60. Morrison might have turned out a cranky megalomaniac and Janis a nutty old hag. But when we look at the contemporaries like Ravi Shanker, Eric Clapton, Paul McCartney, Rolling Stones and Carlos Santana we can't help but think about the lost promises. However, that is a very calculative view of some extraordinary lives. They lived fast and died hard, therein rests the key to our nostalgia for them.

Eric Clapton: Dazzling with Depth

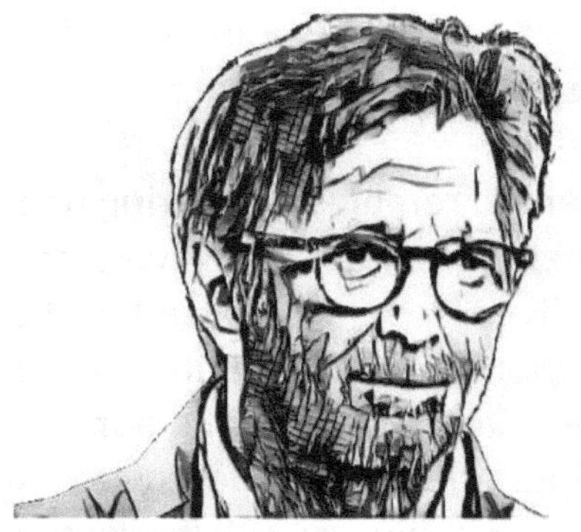

Eric Clapton and his fellow music gods, who are still surviving- Santana, Dylan or Rolling Stones are living affirmation of life giving properties of music. These enduring treasures survived excesses of monumental proportion with luck, talent and above all a rare survival intelligence. Their continued presence on planet Earth can be attributed to divine talent and divine grace in equal measures. There was no reason why they should not have gone the ways of 3 Js Jimi Hendrix, Jim Morrison and Janis Joplin — Bruvera Sparks of raw talent which burnt wildly, only to be extinguished before their 28th birthday in every case. Nostalgic and dark iconography apart, predominant thought is — What a waste!. The sense of loss is more acute when we see the new frontiers explored by their contemporaries like Clapton, Santana or Dylan. They all benefited with new mediums like MTV, Streaming or YouTube. Imagine what Jimi Hendrix would have given us in more than half a century since his death.

Eric Clapton too, appeared to be the perfect case for such a fiery early end. Considered to be a 'God' when he was hardly 20 years of age, Clapton partook, with total abandon, all the excesses that his rock god status and his intoxicating times threw at him. He did 'knock at heaven's door' quite a few times with health scares abound. Divine grace came to him in the form of a survival epiphany. In the throes of psychedelic delirium and alcoholic haze, he was given, what he termed, 'grace of despair'. He clearly recognized that he has an addictive, obsessive and restless personality. For him "the best party in town was always down the road". He wrote in his autobiography about "an obsessive enthusiasm that tended to fade as soon as the desired object was in his possession". He simply couldn't settle, both from the point of view of substance use or musical personality. There was no attainment of cruising altitude of identity, "not with the Yardbirds, who, in effect, sacked him, nor with John Mayall's Bluesbreakers, nor with Cream or Blind Faith. Ever restless, he seems a peevish character always in pursuit of the next let down." Great thing was that he was aware of this defect and had enough wherewithal and timber in his soul to tackle that to his advantage when the time arrived. This clarity saved him. His music or his life or his general outlook were formed by dealing with the dynamics of this lacune and clear realization of its mortal implications. This handling of obsession and restlessness is the guiding feature of his musical journey also. Dispassionate acceptance has become his default stance- measured and unruffled, much like his playing.

His ability to stay with an obsession just up to the edge of the precipice kept him in the dark zone long enough to reap the benefits of corrosive depths of psychedelic chasm of the addiction or the intricacies of the music that appear in the heightened throes of chemically induced chaos. At the same time his ability to retract in time and realize the virtue of sobriety were a sign of absence of arrogance and acceptance of his vulnerability. This mellowed, somewhat diffident self-regard, so unlike rock gods of the time, was the reason for his survival. This also enabled the variety and commercial viability of his musical output. Despite initial Blues fanaticism, he was not stubborn and was willing to bend his musical purity to the demands of audience and commercial tastes. When he recorded the album 'Behind The Sun in Montserrat' in 1985, the recording label found it substandard and said this much to his face. His reaction explains much of his personality and his music. "Instead of getting arrogant and outraged, I did the shrewd thing," he said. He agreed to a "new, more middle-of-the-road style that was not to the taste of many of his old blues friends'. He knew what he was doing and was conflicted about it but he was clear about the requirement of survival. "I felt like I was selling out," he said in an interview. But the dividend was rich, not only in terms of record sales but also in expansion of the range. This Blues puritan has a body of work which includes Blues, hard rock, Reggae (I shot the sheriff), Ballads (Tear in the sky, You look wonderful tonight) and a whole lot of middle-of-the-road 'sell out' stuff which led to a guilty conscience and phenomenal record sales.

His tribulations with his addictions and obsessions have left him a well-rounded personality. A musical tool devoid of ego, who could easily play sideman to much junior artists, A doyan who would not be averse to be known for his covers of others, a superstar figure who will never be afraid to be a fanboy, a purist in some pursuits who will not consider any music taboo and above all a seasoned debauch who will be comfortable with his domesticated edginess. It is a mark of a real 'God' to relinquish the 'God' status and feel relieved.

His musical identity is so rich that some critics, bred on recognizable but singular, hooks of titans, found him devoid of identity. A summation of his skills on his 70th birthday explains the process beautifully- "All these different guitarists would have their famous five licks, and Clapton learned them all. He mastered those early blueprints to perfection, so he had a dozen licks, then two dozen, and he would link them all up on the pentatonic blues scale in ways that gave him almost unlimited twists and wiggles, played utterly heroically." Here is a musical identity that has not been chiseled by limitation but formed by ever growing abundance.

It is very easy to be deceived by his subdued style. He has sedate demeanour and a musical style that aims to dazzle with depth then with antics. Eric Clapton has played with each and every big name from Hendrix, Page, Beck, Beatles, Frank Zappa, BB King, Buddy Guy, Rolling Stones and many collaborations with newer talents. He respected raw talents like Handrix and his band mate Duane Allman. He himself, however, has been a less spectacular but deeper talent. His improvisations don't come from Jazz-like 'on the toes' inspirations. He brings "that indefinable extra twist of fluidity" by amassing excellence. It is less showy but much deeper as it comes from years of imbibing music rather than from some innate raw spark. He very astutely recognized this. When asked to comment on the John Laughlin's lament that he (Laughlin) can't play everything that he can think, Eric Clapton said "I'm probably the opposite of John, in that he can probably think of things he wants to play and can't, and I can't think of anything at all! My playing far outreaches my ability to play what I can think. That's why I could never be a jazz musician, because I can't hear it in my head. I play from somewhere else, where it simply goes to my hands." He is a player of massive depth, his innovations come from reiteration and going deeper and farther. The novelty emerges from the piling of the existing. He has succeeded as one, perhaps more accurate assessment, says "Mr. Clapton seems to have an open channel between his guitar and his inner feelings that neither age nor imitation can cut off." He might not be aiming to dazzle but the reservoir of pure music and collision of myriad influences create startling moments routinely.

It is easy to be duped and think that his music is all technique and artistry and no soul. He has stayed invested in polishing his craft and art as it has been a means of communication and healing. He communicated his sorrow, heartbreak and despair over his crippling addiction through music. Layla, Tear in the Heaven are case in point. Talking about his trials Eric Clapton said "I knew intuitively that if I played it would medicate me and calm me. The biggest problem was that I didn't know what to think or feel and I went into a numb zone, which is the body defending itself because madness beckons in these situations. The only way to keep myself afloat was to play, I had a guitar in my hands all day until I went to sleep." His music saves him, props him and propels him. "When I'm playing well, what is there to fear? In the moment, there is nothing to fear. Music, when you give it that opportunity, hammers that home." This patrician with scholarly looks has an abyss of despair that gave his music a terrifying depth and a bracing poise. This led to a natural affinity with the Blues.

Eric Clapton defines Blues as "true music of the soul, without the intellect." He pioneered the British interest in the Southern American music of black plantation workers. He got initiated into music by the work of Muddy Waters and his ilk. To a loner teenager with a complicated family life (illegitimate son of a teenage mother, raised by grandparents thinking his mother to be his sister for a long time) Blues gave a solace. A tormented soul that recognized the sadness in the music. The Blues is a dialogue of "of redemption, of suffering and joy". It will help to quote at length from a Guardian article on his 70th birthday that talks of his early journey and how accumulation of knowledge, art and influences creates a unique style. Clapton tells the writer "in England we were bombarded with pop more than anything else, You had to consciously steer a path towards black soul or blues. Most of the players in the rock framework were coming from a rockabilly stance. Jimmy Page and Jeff Beck grew up listening to white guitar players like Scotty Moore and Cliff Gallup. I was obsessed with black blues guitar players, and for me the ultimate problem was trying to shift that style into a Chuck Berry rock format." Clapton continues "Blues is a language you have to learn, like learning French. It's not about a feeling, it's an action. There's a lot to learn and it means going to the library and listening to just about everything that was ever done and trying to learn from that." The coming lines explain the magic of innovation by accumulation. "And then something happens. If you do your work and do your best to carry the burden of the past and the fellowship of the blues, so you know you've done all your research and you've studied everything you can, I think if you really love the music you'll start to express it your own way. It's almost impossible not to." At another place he has written that he finds his stability in the blues, the music that he first loved and that he continues to regard as a kind of beacon. "There's a matter-of-factness, a sense of acceptance about the blues". Eric Clapton's 1994 'From the Cradle' is the best selling traditional blues recording in history.

His personality, style and mood that have been framed over a long period, have served him well in his late years. His post MTV unplugged (1992) journey is a saga of relentless creativity. In the new millennium he brought out good music in Albums (Riding with the King, Me and Mr. Johnson, Back Home, The Road to Escondido, The Breeze), tours and various events like Crossroads, a festival dedicated to guitar, tribute to George Harrison and many more. Today, Eric Clapton is a beacon and a servant of music. He has adroitly avoided the prima donna title of elder statesman of music and stays relevant. He found relevance lies in staying a student forever rather than being a monument. He is playing with a depth of life, which many say, wasn't there in 1966. He is active, learning and at peace with himself.

Eric Clapton provides a very cogent summation of his musical journey in his autobiography. "My musical identity has taken my entire life to develop,now I can sing in a band, play backup, lead, sing a duet — there doesn't have to be a label on it anymore. The most important thing is that I enjoy listening to music, and I still do." He continues "acceptance is a great state of being. It steps aside of hysteria, drama, extreme emotions." It is this side-stepping of extreme emotions by living them and leaving them, Clapton has created an enduring excellence of poised and unblinking sensibility.

Carlos Santana: Sensual Spirituality of a Monk

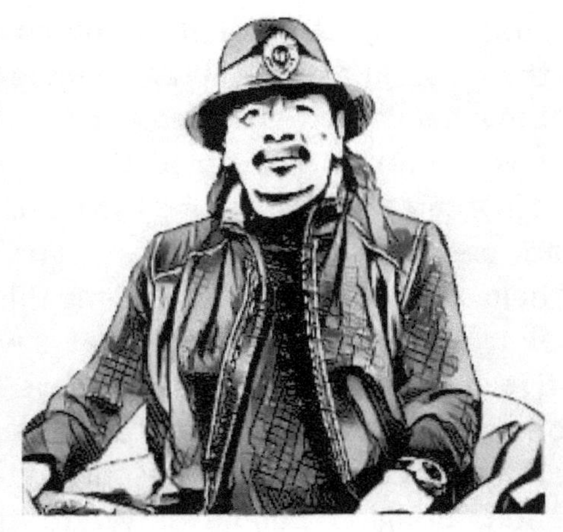

Carlos Santana understands the utility of a little bit of sin in life. He had the opportunity to experience sacred and profane early in his life. He was initiated in music via violin, which he played in the church. Later, when he shifted to guitar, he was playing in strip clubs in the Mexican border town of Tijuana. His spirituality has rightly been called his muse and the supreme achievement of his spirituality has been to harness the sensual to the service of music. Music for him is something that changes people's molecular structure. One single note and it changes the way people feel.

Coming back to the sacred and profane, he once told Rolling Stone that in church you play the music in a certain way, "people just fold their hands and go wherever they go; when you work in a strip joint, you play music in a certain way, and it's like watching a black panther when it's in heat." For him "the halo and the horns are the same thing... it is ok to be spiritually horny – that is what creative genius is really about". He says "I'm curious about how to penetrate inside the note. I want to utilize sound, resonance, and vibration, bringing people closer to their own heart". Obviously, we are dealing with a flower child of the 60's, out to transform fear on this planet into light and love. In him, for a change we find a person, a musician who has learnt to utilize the excesses of his era and profession to enhance his creativity. He endures, as he knows how to "upgrade his software into something more illuminating." Above all he learnt the difference between getting loaded and getting high well in time when his contemporaries were self-destructing themselves all around him on drugs. He may have looked like a relic in the early 90's but his forte - spirituality and sensuality never went out of style and he stays popular across generations.

Invitation to have good time

Rock as a music form, had energy, anguish and a level of beautiful noise that has sustained it over the ages. Blues tradition brought in a soul and Jazz a whimsy that became a rollicking lilting element in the somewhat harsh landscape of rock. There were attempts to bring in the rhythmic vitality of African, Latin and Indian music. As those were the times when giants decided to descend on planet earth in bunches, many good attempts were made. Leading lights like Ravi Shankar, George Harrison, Laughlin of Mahavishnu and Bob Marley did a fairly good job of bringing these sounds from far away lands and joyous sensibilities that pulsated in these music traditions. However, somehow, all that never came together in a sustained and sustainable manner. These efforts never could shed their exotic feel. It was left to Carlos Santana to close the loop through his cosmopolitan sensibilities rooted in exuberant Latin rhythm.

Carlos Santana is the central force of his band called, well, Santana. Bill Graham was an early promoter who mentored the young band. He has the best explanation about why Santana succeeded as opposed to somewhat vapid and ghettoised earlier efforts. I will quote at length. Bill Graham says "What impressed me is that it was an attempt at fusing rock and Afro and Latino and getting a rhythmic sensuous sound into rock, which I've always thought it lacked in many cases." Graham goes on to lay down the sensuality of early Santana which holds real even today. "What it is, is an earthy street thing when it really gets up-tempo. You want to move and it's physical. I like dancing together. And Latin music — part of Latin music for me always — was I would hold a woman, and I would touch her body, and we would sweat, and it's all of that … very sensual, very sensuous." Santana has evolved and got enriched by collaboration with varied and younger sounds. This exuberant sensuality remains.

Black Magic Woman, an early hit, starts with a gripping chord on keyboard and soon Carlos takes over with his silken guitar licks and takes the music to a different level.

Percussions create a trance and very soon the song becomes a voodoo dance of seduction and abandon of love. The number can rouse a stadium even today after more than forty years. A truly timeless classic.

Carlos Santana echoes Bill Graham when he talks about the 'Smooth' perhaps his most famous Latin single. Santana explained in an interview, "When people hear 'Smooth,' it's boogie," Santana says. "It's an invitation to have a good time. Like Little Richard used to say: It's Friday night, I got a little bit of money, I did my homework, and it's OK to rub closely with Sally or Sue; she gave me that look like it's OK. I brushed my teeth, and I got deodorant. I got her going. It's cool. Certain songs — 'Smooth,' 'Oye Como Va,' 'Guantanamera,' 'La Bamba,' the 'Macarena,' 'Louie Louie' — that's what these songs are for."

Santana, as an elderly statesman of Woodstock generation, retains a bracing forthrightness harking back to the times when giving good time to a woman was not considered so politically sensitive. At fourteen he was playing in strip clubs of Tijuana and was learning to play guitar in a way, as he accepted later, with a serene equanimity, 'so that women's nipples would go hard'. This feat apart, Carlos has displayed an old fashioned respect for women, a respect that, on a deeper analysis, is far more meaningful than the politically correct platitudes. Women are not only a source of his creativity but also a touchstone of his creative output. In an interview Santana said, "women are really supremely important for musicians. We all learn from how they walk, how they talk. It's not politically correct today, but in the old days, in the Sixties, if somebody was an incredible musician, you'd say, 'He's a bitch,' and if he was an incredible musician but he has a lot of class and style, then you'd say, 'Oh, he's a lady.'" One needs to cut him some slack on the PC front and understand where the sentiment is coming from. Apart from the appreciation of women, he is really elated when his music gets feminine validation. He explains his impact "when I move around in the music, is to make sure that the bass, drums and keyboards are on the one. That creates the trance, the spell. And it makes women go absolutely wild." His friend, sometime Mahavishnu Orchestra drummer Narada Michael Walden, made Santana write a guajira (a style of Cuban music, song or dance). That's how he explained the form in the presence of the guitar maestro. "Guajira is the most effective way to, excuse the expression, penetrate a woman's heart and then they remember the whole glory of being a female and start dancing a certain way. It's the most tried, true and tested frequency that makes women open up like a flower." Basically, for Santana, music needs to celebrate womanhood. Some sentences may appear tasteless to the ear in 2019 but no doubt, the explanations are coming from a place of respect, appreciation and love.

School of Hard Knocks

Born in 1947 in Jalisco, Mexico, Carlos Santana had a musical upbringing as his father was a mariachi violinist. Young Carlos joined his father in the street playing for small change. His first instrument was violin. This beginning is often seen as the cause of his sustained long notes. He played violin in the church choir also. Very soon he shifted to guitar. He told in an interview that even in those early days "I had my ear on Chuck Berry, Little Richard and Bo Diddley, on B.B. King and T-Bone Walker. There was nothing plastic about those guys. They went deep, and each note carried something important. I knew, from a long time ago, the difference between notes and life. I'd rather play life than notes." Another early school was the rough-and-tumble of Tijuana. There, an adolescent Carlos started getting work in shady night clubs playing from four in the afternoon until six in the morning, one hour on, then one hour off, while the strippers stripped. This was a tough life but the young musician was content. He resisted his mother's determined efforts to migrate to the USA. Finally, the family moved to San Francisco's Spanish-speaking Mission district in 1961.

Carlos got a fertile environment in the 60s Bay Area. Psychedelic underground and anti-Vietnam war protests on the social political front and new trends in the field of music were the suitable diet for the raw talent that was Carlos Santana. With organist Gregg Rolie he assembled the first Santana band. They were lucky to catch the eye of Bill Graham who helped their appearance at many important venues, most notably, Fillmore West concert hall and 1969 Woodstock. Graham ensured that they figured in the film and the album made on the iconic Woodstock event arguably the condensed crystallization of the spirit of the 60s.

Guardian writes, "Carlos's earliest musical idols had been bluesmen like Muddy Waters, Buddy Guy and Otis Rush, but he began to listen to a more diverse palette of sounds. To the basic rock and blues base, Santana added Latin rhythms and the freer shapes of modern jazz, absorbed from records like John Coltrane's My Favourite Things and Miles Davis's rock-jazz fusion, Bitches Brew. Santana's first albums - up to and including the fourth, the complex, jazz-inflected Caravanserai of 1972 - were some of the most original and powerful of their time." A consistent performer, in a career spanning half a century Santana has sold more than 100 million records and has carved a unique niche for himself. As 2014 release of Corazón, was received well, Santana surpassed the Rolling Stones and is one of only two music acts in Billboard history to score at least one Top Ten album for six consecutive decades from the 1960s on.

Rhythm Divine

Even in his early Interviews, Santana Showed signs of deep spirituality. However with success, his spirituality blossomed. It is very easy to be dismissive of his spiritual jargon. However, as you know more about the person, a feeling grows that in Carlos Santana we are dealing with a person who has cracked it. His exotic sounding spiritual paraphernalia is helping him tremendously in staying creative and rooted. Introducing him as one the greatest guitarist of all times, Rolling Stone magazine has summed up saying "Santana has remained a compelling musician with a devotional spirituality fueling his muse." In the early seventies he and his first wife became followers of the Indian Guru Shri Chinmoy. He was very close to similarly spiritual jazz musicians, including John McLaughlin, Stanley Clarke, Wayne Shorter and Herbie Hancock. He is deeply grateful for those years of spiritual guidance when he went by the name 'Devadip' the divine lamp/light, turned vegan and followed monkish discipline. He developed spiritually, however, by 1981, he started outgrowing his guru and embarked on a journey of finding his own way.

Chris Heath did the last cover story of the Rolling Stone Magazine on Carlos Santana. He saw his 'church' and talked about his interaction with 'angles'. He concluded, "I am, by nature, probably more cynical than most, but all I can tell you is that when he talks about this stuff, it doesn't seem kooky or unhinged or even that spacey. Likewise, in all the time I spend with Carlos Santana, I see no signs that he is unaware of life's mundane realities." With his music, his success, his longevity and his serene visage the entire spiritual edifice feels credible. He is acutely aware that people may get uneasy when he goes on spiritual tangent. He is also clear that this unease doesn't bother him. He told Heath "My reality is that God speaks to you every day. It is just an inner voice, and you trust it. That voice will never take you to the desert." He shares that the angles tell him to be gracious, grateful and patient. He lives by what he thinks is his reality and that has held him in good stead. It is pointless to question the physical veracity of his notions. One thing is certain that he is positive, joyful and totally devoid of deceit about his beliefs. That should do.

Carlos Santana is one of the last greats standing and thriving from the creative ferment of a very exciting times. He gives us a chance to touch the heady sixties and presents a least destructive but explosively powerful facet of the flower-power days. He cobbled, perhaps, a more illustrious second innings than the original one. His music is based on his raw talent and capability of bringing a delicious chaos together in accessible music. A music that begets joy or, as he says, connects molecules to light. We, mortals, will be best served by being grateful and open to the miracle that is Carlos Santana.

Rolling Stones: So That We Can All Grow Old Disgracefully

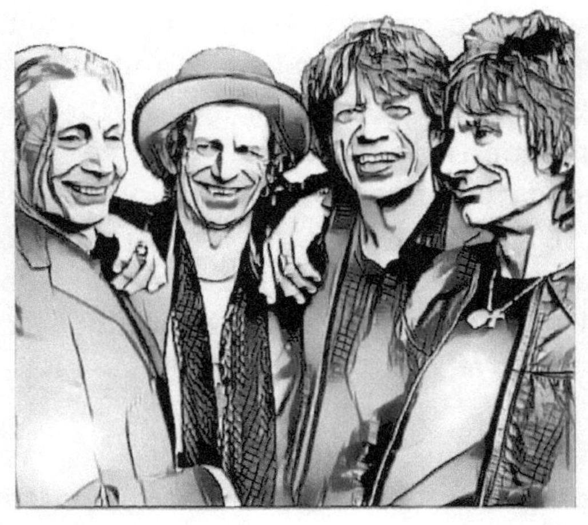

Life and times of Rolling Stone are a living, breathing and very vivid representation of Rock & Roll itself. In Rolling Stone we can see how archetypes are formed. Something posits itself in public imagination because it mirrors reality of a phenomenon in its all pulsating details. Rolling Stones are the origin, zenith and mainstreaming (with its unavoidable mellowing) of Rock & Roll. They embody the influences, main themes and growth path of one of the most exciting chapters of the history of Music-i.e. Rock & Roll. More than that, they ARE the tradition of Rock & Roll. Rock & Roll has come of age accumulating influences from fringes becoming a big river. This collision of many strands like country, blues, beat poetry, funk and R&B created a rich repertoire of new musical idioms which a turbulent generation made its own. In the process, it traded a bit of its churlish rebelliousness and most of its innocence for maturity of seasoned world weariness and elegant debauchery. This is Rock & Roll and also a pen portrait of Rolling Stone.

Rock & Roll couldn't find a more appropriate totem. The Stones' endurance remains a key factor. Rock and Roll has its romance in early deaths of its leading light. Loss of Jimi Hendrix, Janis Joplin, Jim Morrison and later Kurt Cobain are cases in point. However, in final analysis, the tradition of Rock and Roll needs the consolidation provided by its inexorable albeit slow march towards maturity. For this, players with enduring presence were needed. That is why, if the allure of rock mythology got its flashy hooks in the blazing but short lived torrents of talent, their iconography was consolidated by the survivors like Eric Clapton, Carlos Santana and perhaps most representatively by Rolling Stone.

This is not to overlook Rolling Stone's own share of untimely demises. One of the original members and arguably, the most adventurous of the lot, Brian Jones was lost to the excesses of the era. Some credit Jones with christening the band as Rolling Stones as he took it from a Muddy Waters song. Jones was extremely reckless and had a history to prove it. He had fathered two illegitimate children before he was 16. He had his moments in the notable 1968 album 'Beggars Banquet'. Rolling Stone magazine says that Jones had "lent sitar, dulcimer, and, on "Under My Thumb," marimba to the band's sound, and who had been in Morocco recording nomadic Joujouka musicians." The Magazine also comments "Brian, never a day at the beach in the human-being department, was increasingly lost as a musical presence, but he has his final great moments on 'Beggars Banquet'. When Brian plays a ghostly slide guitar on "No Expectations," he sounds like he's playing at his own funeral." He was given the boot by the band on June 9, 1969 and was found dead in his swimming pool on July 3, 1969. Drugs proved to be his undoing. Coroner called it 'death by misadventure' not a very rare occurrence in the era that saw many leading lights succumbing to such misadventures.   Jones also appeared on 'Let it Bleed' released a day after his burial.

Notwithstanding the loss of Jones, Rolling Stones is a study in permanence. Their survival in itself is a great achievement. More creditably, they have kept the wheels moving and regeneration by creation had been their motif in their splendid innings of half a century (still counting). Even in abeyance their creative juices kept flowing and kept the rolling stone saga lubricated and functioning. Impending doom was always looming but gradually that became a permanent fixture and hovering doom was a reassuring sign the bad boys were at work. Their longevity ensured that they remained "a scandalous symbol of 'generational independence", says Peter Conrad in a not so flattering half century review of the band. He adds "now that we baby boomers are too rickety to do much dancing, the stones serve as precious relic of our teenage days.

Encouraged by them we can all grow old disgracefully."
Despite the death of drummer Charlie Watts in 2021, The group is still filling stadiums and 81 year old Mick Jagger is still prancing around on stages all over the world as if it is still 1968.

One of the reasons for this peerless survival is given by the bands co-frontsman and guitarist Keith Richards. The explanation is in keeping with his reputation for making his body a lab for all sort of substances. Richards was never self-destructive despite all the evidence to the contrary. In his autobiography 'Life' he helpfully explains that 'he never succumbed to the rock star archetype of early death because he used only the "finest, finest cocaine and the purest, purest heroin." Richard Corliss of Time Magazine was having a great time while reviewing the autobiography- "Keith Richards has been the subject of many lurid rumors; most of them turn out to be understatements…… Life does contain enough drug tales to fill Thomas de Quincy's Confessions of an English Opium Eater — from Richards' description of a 1972 bust in Arkansas, where dope was concealed not just in the folds of his cap but also in his car's side panels, through his helpful delineation of barbiturates ("the sensible drugs in the world are the pure ones"), to his awed evocation of LSD: "There's not much you can say about acid except, God, what a trip!"

One thanks the gods of Rock and Roll for the quality consciousness of Stones. However, on a more serious note, Stones have endured for so long because of their fidelity to their roots. Stripped of all the trappings of hype and fame, Rolling Stones is basically a very solid blues band. Rhythm & Blues was their initial passion which matured into uncanny mastery. The most instantly recognizable Stones riff has been the wail and gloom of blues. "The reason the Stones have endured so long as the World's Greatest Rock-and-Roll Band, of course, is their ability to consistently make music that remains true to their blues and R & B roots while at the same time assimilating new musical sounds and stamping them as their own. By now, they have built up such an impressive body of work that they could easily deliver shows made up of nothing but greatest hits, but the band has refused to become a nostalgia act" Wrote Michiko

Kakutani of New York Times. "The Stones' pirate-like swagger, their unsentimental view of sex, their shimmering ballads of longing and loss are all rooted in the blues tradition, as are their gritty, unvarnished meditations on love and death -- qualities that help explain why even the band's earliest work, unlike the more pastel-colored love songs of the Beatles, has so defiantly endured…… iconography that ratifies the music's haunting ambiguities, its ecstatic, Dionysian groove" adds the former Chief Book Critic of the Times.

Blues has life enhancing properties. For many of its practitioners it has been a lifelong profession. Its regenerative powers have kept giants like Muddy Waters, Buddy Guy and Howling wolf – all icons for the Stones- active into a very long and fruitful careers. Keith Richards' guitar conveys the longings and lyricism of blues tradition with great facility. Jagger told Kakutani "'My kind of writing has always been blues-influenced because it's the music I grew up with, I couldn't really write happy love songs. I was coming from a different standpoint. Lots of double-edged humor and rather dark narratives -- that's all to do with the blues.

Compared to 50's pop, the blues always seemed much more grown-up."

The Stones started with covers of 'Little Red Rooster', 'Love in vain' and other standard Blues anthems to show their grasp over a powerful musical tradition. With 'Midnight Rambler' and 'Satisfaction' they owned by redefining it.

Many critics have decided that Rolling Stone peaked creatively in the mid 1960s and everything since then has been a matter of scrupulous, mercenary, "decline management." Magazine Rolling Stone notes almost admiringly "through the 1980s the group became more an institution than an influential force."

While the recall for the earlier hits like Satisfaction or Honky Tonk Women or Jumpin' Jack Flash is far greater, their later work were also cohesive and realized pieces of dynamic music. Rolling Stone Magazine says "Bridges to Babylon has prime moments, especially Mick's "Might as Well Get Juiced" and Keith's "Thief in the Night." A Bigger Bang was worth the wait, bristling with Mick's snakiest wit, Keith's shrewdest guitar runs, Charlie's loosest drum hooks. From "Rough Justice" to "This Place Is Empty," it's the work of hardened rock & roll dons who don't feel any need to prove a goddamn thing"

Maybe, their fidelity towards blues may be the reason for the accusations of them being creatively stalled in their early hits. However, their longevity is based on their avoiding mindless imitation of their icons. "Perhaps being English, they were less inclined than their American contemporaries to slavish imitation; perhaps being true blues devotees, they instinctively understood the music's emphasis on personal expression." They are content with their sound 'a sound that is classic but it still rocks.' Their later studio album 'Bigger Bang' "does not reinvent the wheel, just rolls it one more time with panache." This means that they were managing bigger feet of performing with great originality in a restricted space. Keith Richards told New York Times "It's easy to play a 12-bar blues anybody can do it -- it's whether it hits home or not. That's the hard thing, because you have to dig deep. You can't slouch the blues, you can't toss it off. Musically, it's a very limited form of music -- three, four chords if you're smart. It's where you place them and how you phrase it and how you sound it. It's a very tight frame to work within, but there's something within that framework that can express more than all the wailing away in the world." True affirmation of their greatness is in the flexibility of their idiom. Once again Kakutani hits the sweet spot "Somewhere along the line, in spreading the gospel of the blues, the Stones discovered their own voice as artists -- an infinitely flexible voice that somehow managed to accommodate modernist irony and postmodernism humor without losing its soul, a voice adept at everything from the surreal portrait ("Get Off of My Cloud") to the elegiac story song ("Memory Motel") to the straight-ahead rock-and-roll anthem ("Jumpin' Jack Flash")." This flexibility can come only with owning the genre and having the confidence to declare with all the "sullen charisma that makes it impossible to take your ear off from it.' The Ferocious nonchalance of Keith Richards and primal restlessness of Mick Jagger should not be allowed to deflect the attention from the growth and movement in their music.

However, there is no doubt that they lost their 'dangerous aura'. Familiarity bred by their long existence has created a companionability that makes us approach them as a 'feel good band'. No wonder they are the most profitable and enduring brand name in the history of Music. Their tours are complete sold out. The 'Bigger Bang' tour of 2005 lasted for two years and grossed $558 million — highest ever for any tour in that era.

The Rolling Stones have definitely cut down on the 'Sympathy for Devil' and have become Voodoo Loungers and Men of Wealth and Taste. Their spark has not diminished and they have not stopped enjoying making great music. Their endurance and success is, in a very big part, due to the very transparent avidity and 'soul hunger' for music. The Alchemy that gets worked up when the musical soul-mates perform on stage is stuff of immortality. Keith Richards captures it too well ""There's a certain moment when you realize that you've actually just left the planet for a bit and that nobody can touch you ……you're elevated because you're with a bunch of guys that want to do the same thing as you.

And when it works, baby, you've got wings.
You are flying without a license."

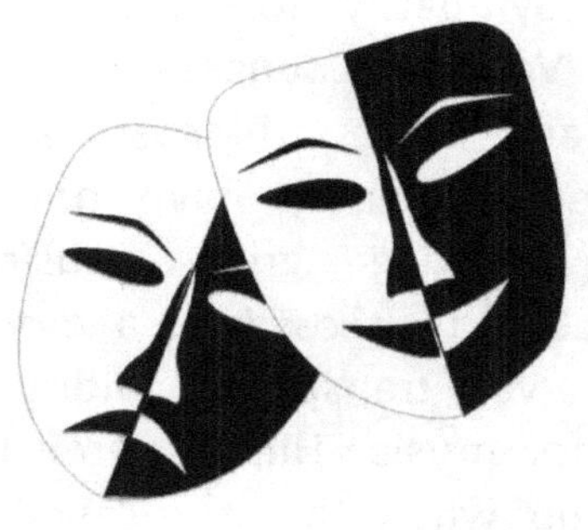

Bob Dylan: Once More For a Simple Twist of Fate

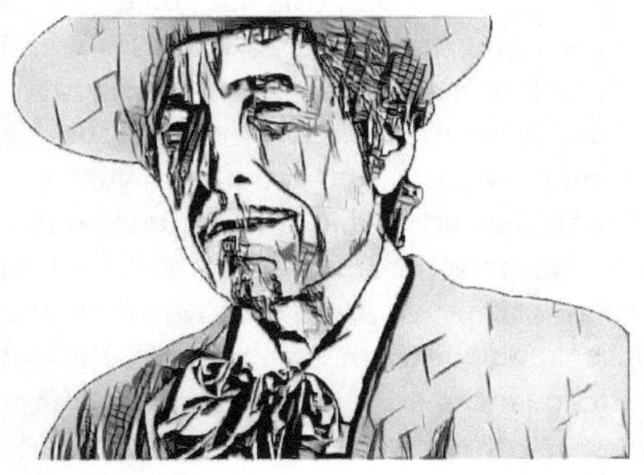

Voice of Bob Dylan has finally gone kaput. This is from no less an authority than the Wall Street Journal. Well, maybe so. But part of the fun with stalwarts is their teasing promises of resurgence. This voice- "the voice of a rogue ageless in decrepitude" has for long been making insidious forays into the landscape of music and stomping various strands of art forms into its own image. Bob Dylan, who is in his eighties, continues to tour for almost one third of the year to a rousing reception. The artist in the ninth decade of life, has been described aptly as "the Methuselah of righteous cool" but he has been much more, a master of disdain now, a bard of decay only to surprise as a voice of longing for romance later. The elderly statesman of music has collided with forms ranging from folk to glam rock and many in between and has left them richer, altered forever. In every endeavour he opened new gates and redefined what can be treated as art. Dylan the unquestionable 'poet laureate' of rock, with a Nobel in literature to prove it, started with folk and transcended the form by owning it. He lent poetic nuances to the protest movement that was shrieking around him in the early sixties. He was the reluctant hero who was seen as the voice of his times. Since then he has been conducting a ceaseless and successful campaign to break one rock archetype after another. From sincere country folk singer to protest singer to rock & roll star in its all shimmering razzmatazz to religious evangelist to witty old man to wistful singer of lost love, Dylan has been leaving his followers stranded in his astonishingly varied footprints during his half a century long career.

Only a pure artist will work with such a matter-of-fact fury to dismantle the image which may potentially throttle his growth as an artist. Bob Dylan tasted extreme fame at an early age and has been the centre of adoration of millions since his 20s. He is supposed to have said "Just because you like my stuff doesn't mean I owe you anything." He was the pioneer among the breed of real artists who refused to be defined by their audience. His disrespect for his followers' expectation may look arrogant but he is about staying true to his creative urge and communicating it with relentless invention. In one of rare attempts to explain himself he said "I don't want to get harsh and say I don't care. You do care, you care in a big way, otherwise you wouldn't be there. But it's a different kind of connection. It's not a light thing." Critic Jonathan Letham wrote in 2006 "Puncturing myths, boycotting analysis and ignoring chronology are likely part of a long and lately quite successful campaign not to be incarcerated within his own legend. Dylan's greatest accomplishment since his Sixties apotheosis may simply be that he has claimed his story as his own."

Bob Dylan's towering musical presence should not be allowed to obscure the fact that he is primarily a songwriter. He made his breakthrough as a singer-songwriter who expanded the limited confines of folk protest singing. His first album 'Bob Dylan (1962)' contained only two originals. With his exquisite sense of timing Dylan forged a career that was both timely and transcending. He saw the pointlessness of singing other people's songs and tapped his own poetic reservoir. Answer came "blowin' in the wind". His next album 'The Freewheelin' Bob Dylan (1963)' was a torrent of poetry which was both accessible and elusive at the same time. "Blowin' in the Wind", "Masters of War" soon acquired anthem-like status. "A Hard Rain's a-Gonna Fall" fell directly on the collective psyche of a generation for which nuclear holocaust was a palpable possibility. Immediately he was lapped up as the official balladeer of the civil rights movement. 'The Times They Are a-Changin (1964)' had plain but haunting protest songs like "The Lonesome Death of Hattie Carroll" and the title track. Young Dylan added poetry and panache to the folk idiom. He enriched the simpler form and made it appealing to those who had taste for a bit of complexity. His stinging nasal voice lent authenticity to his great songs. Heightened social consciousness of the 60's allowed him to retain the popular base despite an uppity taste in lyrics.

In an ideologically charged atmosphere, this popularity bred fanatic rigidity among some of Dylan fans, for whom his symbolism was bigger than his music. But the 'Napoleon in Rags' had just started to carve his musical identity. His craving-driven musical journey had no place for straitjackets of adoration or even the constraints of a genre. In 'The Times They Are a-Changin' itself, we find one of the better break-up songs, "Boots of Spanish Leather." He gave a teaser for moving towards sonic density by excellent sniggering ballads full of lilting sway of seducer like "Spanish Harlem Incident" then showing his lurid sensuality in "It Ain't Me Babe". Followers of a clean-cut voice of zeitgeist were beginning to get confused but the majority were rubbing their hands in glee.

Summer of 65 was nigh. It was the apogee of rock when in the course of one and half years Dylan came out with "Bringing It All Back Home" (March, 1965), "Highway 61 Revisited" (August), and the double album "Blonde on Blonde" (May, 1966). This was the time when the Beatles were unleashing "Help" (August, 1965), "Rubber Soul" (December, 1965), and "Revolver" (August, 1966). Blessed were those who were young during this orgy of pure talent. With 'Bringing It All Back Home (1965)' Dylan stayed acoustic but the other side was electric. Howls and cheers rose in unison. However the musician was on a feverish roll to notice all that. He was busy creating magic. This is how 'Rolling Stone' Magazine describes the album "On the electric first side, Dylan sneered his absurdist, word-drunk rambles over lean, jittery garage rock, brimming over with wild humor, while side two had four brain-frazzling acoustic ballads that made The Times They Are a-Changin' sound like kid stuff." 'Highway 61 Revisited' consolidated his reputation as poet of the rock with "all doomy menace and hallucinatory wit, packing a career's worth of rock & roll innovation into each of the nine songs. " The album had "Like a Rolling Stone," a #2 hit in 1965. Later it was voted the most influential song ever. Poet was in full bloom in "Tombstone Blues," "Ballad of a Thin Man," and the epic , complex "Desolation Row." The Juggernaut rolled on and came 'a surreal fever dream of a record', double-vinyl 'Blonde on Blonde.' The record concluded the coronation of the king of rock. 15 months preceding Blonde on Blonde, witnessed the most intense burst of creativity any rock & roller has ever had. Such good deeds don't go unpunished.

A ravaged, burnt out Dylan went and crashed his motorcycle and managed to get away to straighten himself up. Many were sceptical about the excuse. That was July 29, 1966. He came back to album making with 'John Wesley Harding (1968)' that had gems like "All Along the Watchtower" (more famous as a cover by Jimi Hendrix). 1969 had 'Nashville Skyline' with his honey-dipped, smoking free voice. "Lay Lady Lay" was a pleasant reminder that the master was at helm. These were the precursors of his first stay in the "valley of suckdom". Indifferent Albums and a collection of writing received lukewarm response. He was selling well, continuously giving good songs but they were sporadic and hidden deep in ordinary albums. His Pat Garrett soundtrack had the hit "Knockin' on Heaven's Door." Then out of nothing came a resounding affirmation of his genius in the form of a perfect album 'Blood on the Tracks (1975)'. Starting with "Tangled

Up in Blue," the album had iconic meditations on lost love ("Idiot Wind", "If You See Her, Say Hello"). It was a great comeback but was followed by long average performances in the late 70's and 80's, a period that saw more downs than ups. He turned to occult and evangelism starting from Street legal (1978) to a brief return to form in 1983's Infidels. He was active, touring and recording but signs of decline were there as efforts were not comparable to anything Dylan. However there was a third wind in store and came a proper masterpiece in 'Time Out of Mind (1997). The Album" shocked the world because it didn't even echo past glories—it was a ghostly, beautiful new sound, yet another side of Bob Dylan." Opening song 'love sick' informed the world that Dylan had a new trick up his sleeve for his battered voice. It was a new sound world weary, down with sceptic sneer but given the right treatment, capable of transmitting devastatingly condensed emotions. He completed the hat-trick of masterpieces with Love and Theft (2001) and Modern Times (2006). In 2001 he was honoured with an Oscar for original song for Michel Douglas starrer 'Wonder Boys'. The song 'things have changed' captures the craving aimlessness of mid-life crisis with uncanny accuracy and without sacrificing the seductive appeal of a loser. These late achievements are the testimony of his enduring genius, his self-reinvention. He showed that he is a student in search and service of music and all his ordinary creations should not lull anyone as they may turn out to be stepping stones in the journey that is Dylan.

It is easy to say that his best work came before his motorcycle accident in 1966. It is said that he achieved more in five years between the age of 20 and 25 than in years after that. It's a tempting proposition as in those years; arguably, he mattered to more people in the deepest possible way than anyone else in the history of music. He reprogrammed the trajectory of popular music. Took people to folk and protest singing then transcended them by infusing the forms with new sensations. Lent intellectual credibility to rock & roll. He laid down new rules about what can be sung, written or played and how. He lifted the floodgates and showed the possibilities for artists to come. His 'protest songs' have been venerated as idioms of consciousness and slipped into language almost as clichés. While all this is true, Dylan is not Dylan just because of those five years. He is not just the 'last moving target of the dream that was '60s rock', he is the chronicle of musical sensitivities 60s onwards. Jimi Hendrix may have been a more pungent tornado of creativity or Jim Morrison was more seductive 'Satan's Seraph' but they did not stay on the stage long enough. Saga of Dylan has been defining in its longevity and continued vitality. Cultural landscape needs patient carving and Dylan had the time. First five years may have been apocalyptic in proportion but real detailing came in the years that followed. Blood on Tracks, Three Masterpieces of this millennium and an Oscar a Nobel and all other not so triumphant albums are part of the journey that by proxy is the journey of popular music.

The poet explorer with his battered rasping voice has been diligently continuing on his path of finding and refining his voice. Even his defeats are uplifting as they were his brash confrontation with the impulse of resting on past laurels. Dylan has continued to surprise with varied hues of his rich musical persona. There is a monk-like persistence in his search for the creative voice. This search has taken him to different musical turfs and has never lapsed into monotonous selling of nostalgia. Not for nothing he has been called 'rock's longest-running font of vitality.' We quiver in anticipation for one more summer in Neverland.

"Only a fool in here would think he's got anything to prove
Lot of water under the bridge, Lot of other stuff too
Don't get up gentlemen, I'm only passing through
People are crazy and times are strange
I'm locked in tight, I'm out of range
I used to care, but things have changed"
-From Bob Dylan's Oscar winning 'Things have changed'

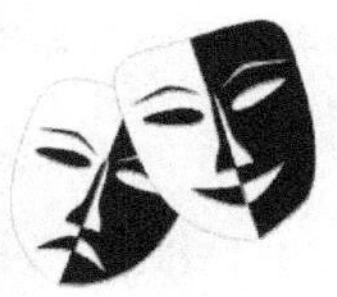

Adele: An unmediated Joy

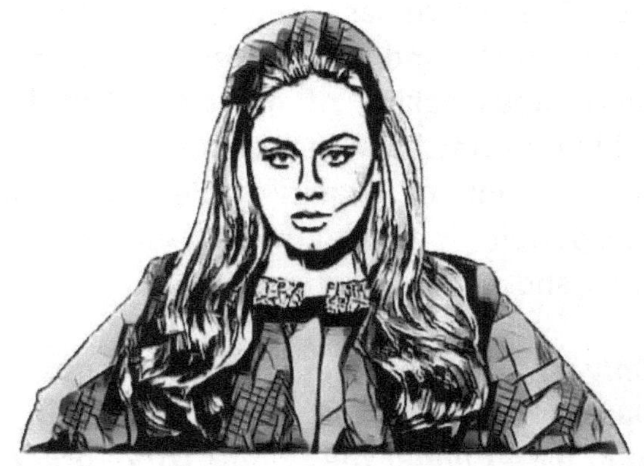

Somehow, it does not feel wrong, a man on the wrong side of fifties, listening to heartbreak songs from a girl of 19, 21 or 25 (though she is much older now). She is pure voice and when Adele sings, such songs are not teen, girly stuff. She infuses those cries, angst and pain with so much classical dignity that it pierces the heart with simple happiness. Not for nothing, her song writing has been compared with Shubert and the Beatles. So the sartorial dignity of yours truly remains uncompromised.

 Elsewhere, while talking about painting, I wrote of Cezanne's 'imperative of solidity'. An artistic output that strives for a solid presence without losing any of its lyricism and suppleness, Adele's songs are solid. She delivers a fully formed concrete reality. Many find her 'incapable of a false note'. Such perfection can turn mechanical, blemishes are life, perfection is stone. There is nothing plastic when she sings.

There may not be any false note but she has that "perfect imperfect voice". A voice that is capable of hitting you with total brutality. Coarse reality living on those notes but fine sensibilities get transmitted through supreme control and superlative vocal skills. The throw and thrum just gets conjured up and stands up in person. Just watch the video of 'Hello' and first 'hello' comes with the burning of the stove-yes, let there be light and there was light.

Her songs convey doubt, uncertainty and yearning but this she does by hitting every note fully — totally bereft of tentativeness. Note comes out fully formed, loud, clear and confident of its purpose. No wobble, no dithering. This direct appeal, this 'unmediated expression, further reinforced by next door, simple English girl persona is a huge part of her appeal. Her voice is not silken but throaty, 'toothsome' throw. It has timber that can carry her frailties and pain with the confidence of a supremely talented youngster.

What has been termed as 'throwback classicism' of her songwriting led to Newyorker slotting her as a "soul singer in the most expansive and truest sense." Songs that are "points of reckoning, reflections, admissions of culpability sung purely and without guile, because what's it matter now?" Adele from her retrospective analysis and regret is able to convey the joy of a relationship with all the attending joy of poetry and music. She can be angry as a youngster or regret some of her behaviour or choices or just stay amazed at the intensity of pain ("They say that time's supposed to heal you, but I ain't done much healing."). Beyond all this artistry is the artist who manages to create musical tsunami at will without surrendering to the demands of the cutthroat world of music industry.

She can afford to bring out albums after a gap of years, say no to tours that sell music, have a combative stance with the streaming services, indulging in a voice destroying eating and drinking habits (though now subdued)and having absolutely non flashy song delivery style ("I just want to sing it. I don't want to perform with my body"). With this she comes back and as a matter of routine nonchalantly collects Grammy, Oscars and sales of millions. This next door girl image adds to her relatability. Audience feels protective about her and when such a person delivers music with such sublime facility, the response is huge. As was said earlier, it is pure voice that hits with its completeness, and comprehensive throw that has made Adele what she is today. Absence of antics is part of this great 'unmediated expression'.

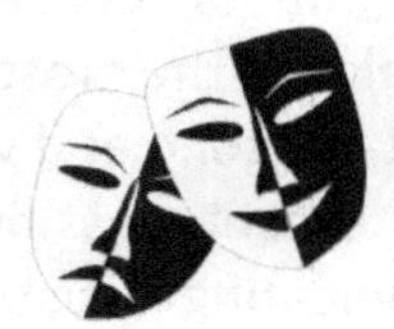

Paul Cezanne: A Moral Imperative of Solidity

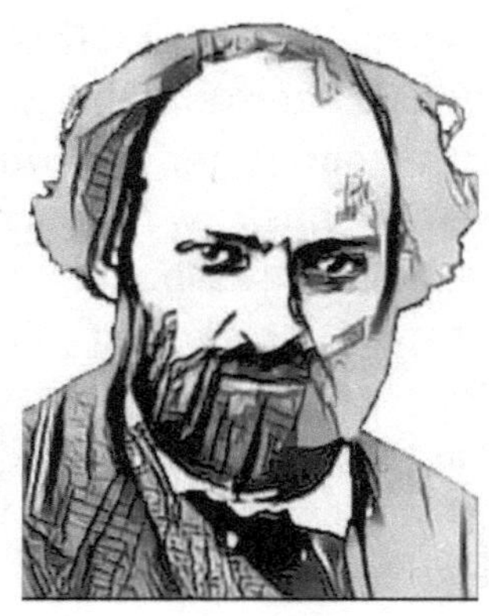

Standing in front of Cezanne canvas is confronting reality in the most clear-cut way. A Cezanne is stark, solid and well defined to the maximum extent possible. In a world where communicating artistic intent in a roundabout way is treated as clever and sublime, Cezanne chose to dig art by conveying presence through solidity. He agonizes 'to realize his sensations'. His sensation is not a fleeting stimulus but a weighted optical whole that has a concrete richness with tangible attributes that challenge the artist to realize them on canvas. Cezanne feels almost a moral imperative to scrupulously realize that presence.

Like his art, Cezanne is a solid presence. There is very little in modern art after him that has not reckoned with him. Cubism may be most open about its debt to Cezanne but Cezanne was 'father of it all' as famously stated by Matisse. When Lucien Freud struggled to bring lardy nakedness out of his portraits, he was facing the same moral imperative of solidity as Cezanne. Even Andy Warhol, in his choice of presentation over representation, was echoing Cezanne. It is common knowledge that his so-called 'geometric works' fed into Cubism. However, it was his meditation on presence that attracted Cubists who, in turn, were also obsessed with bringing out all facets of reality. It is documented that Picasso bought a lithograph of 'Large Bather' when he was working on 'Les Demoiselles d' Avignon.' He was not referring to the 'geometrical works' when he said "it is Cezanne's anxiety that is most interesting." More on this later. Braque was more detailed in his assessment of Cezanne's influence on the movement that he co-founded. Braque said "The discovery of his work overturned everything….I had to rethink everything. There was a battle to be fought against much of what we knew, what we had tended to respect, admire, or love. In Cézanne's works we should see not only a new pictorial construction but also – too often forgotten – a new moral suggestion of space." Pithiness of this observation lies in capturing the moral dimension of Cezanne's obsession.

Coming back to Cezanne's anxiety, this anxiety is a critical part of the moral dimension. In an oft-quoted remark to his son six weeks before his death, Cezanne said "I must tell you that I am becoming, as a painter, more lucid in the presence of nature, but with me, to realize my sensations is always painful. I cannot achieve the intensity that manifests itself to my senses; I do not have the magnificent richness of coloration that animates nature." Cezanne's anxiety- his desperation for expression or a yawning gap between feeling and realization was defined by critic Robert Hughes as ' the scrupulousness of a genius without facility' and was elevated to the level of 'the touchstone of the modern consciousness.'

Hughes too detects the moral dimension in Cezanne's struggle. He writes "his painting was a moral struggle in which the search for identity fused with desire to make the strongest possible images of the other — nature- under the continuous inspiration and abomination of an art tradition that he revered."

Development of Cezanne's art makes for a fascinating reading. His origins had very little art. In Aix-en-Provence, where he was born in 1839 it was as non artistic as was possible in the France of the day. His father was a laborer turned hatter and, eventually, a banker. He (the father) was convinced that his son was not a fool and was surprisingly supportive of his son's artistic plans. From 1852 to 1858 young Cezanne studied humanities at the College Bourbon in Aix, where he met his lifetime friend, Zola the writer. Ironically in college, Cezanne used to win all literary awards and Zola was winner in the arts competitions. After that he studied law for a while, but under Zola's constant encouragement he turned to painting. By 1861 both young men were in Paris.

His fascination with 'presence' found its natural expression in his genius as a portraitist. Starting with an 1869-70 portrait of his painter friend Achille Emperaire he went on to become one of the best portrait artists of all time. His self portraits 'invite comparison with those of Rembrandt, and the best of them justify it'. Like everything Cezanne, his portraits assert their pictorial distinctiveness with every fiber of their being. Subjects of the portrait emerge as 'fully formed' to take their space and cut out any confusion that can lead to dilution of clarity of structures. 'Realization of sensation' is foregrounding of the syntax of presence. Hughes nails Cezanne's pursuit of chiseling out the reality of his local mountain- Mont Ste- Victoire. I will reproduce this biggish paragraph so as not to dilute the astute observations of the critic. "Each painting attacks the mountain and its distance as a fresh problem. The bulk runs from a mere vibration of watercolor on the horizon, its translucent, wriggling profile echoing the pale green and lavender gestures of the foreground trees, to the vast solidarity of the Philadelphia version of Mont Ste.-Victoire, 1902-06. There, all is displacement. Instead of an object in an imaginary box, surrounded by transparency, every part of the surface is a continuum, a field of resistant form. Patches of gray, blue and lavender that jostle in the sky are as thoroughly articulated as those that constitute the flank of the mountain. Nothing is empty in late Cézanne — not even the bits of untouched canvas. …. His goal was presence, not illusion, and he pursued it with an unremitting gravity. The fruit in the great still lifes of the period, like Apples and Oranges, 1895-1900, are so weighted with pictorial decision — their rosy surfaces filled, as it were, with thought — that they seem about twice as solid as real fruit could be. … The light in his watercolors (perhaps the most radiant exercises in that medium since Turner) is not just the transcendent energy, the "supernatural beauty" of abstraction; it is also the harsh, verifiable flicker of sun on Provençal hillsides. To his anguish and fulfillment, Cézanne was embedded in the real world, and he returns us to it, whenever his pictures are seen." It is this struggle of realizing those sensations on canvas that makes Cezanne so enduring.

Durability of Cezanne's appeal is also due to the comprehensive nature of success. He is relatively rare in achieving maturity in multiple aspects of his artistic genius. When his influence on later artists is talked about, mostly the reference is to some particular aspect which was picked by the artists and taken to new heights. In Cezanne we find realization of many aspects- coloration, form, drawing, texture, modeling and expression. His monkish dedication to his art and ability to avoid self-destructive impulses, so common to his era, led to a certain ripeness and heft to his output. This ripeness lent sufficient complexity to his work that enabled later artists to pick and choose from a masterly weave of fully realized fields. Softly dazzling aura of his watercolors, stoic weightiness of his still life or unmistakable 'presence' of his portraits is grand enough to be a foundation of separate schools. Here too, his achievement was embedded in a moral dimension as noted by Meyer Schapiro "he was capable of an astonishing variety. This variety rests on the openness of his sensitive spirit. He admitted to the canvas a great span of perception and mood, greater than that of his Impressionist friends. This is evident from the range of themes alone; but it is clear in the painterly qualities as well. He draws or colors; he composes or follows his immediate sensation of nature; he paints with a virile brush solidly, or in the most delicate sparse watercolor, and is equally sure in both. He possessed a firm faith in spontaneous sensibility, in the resources of the sincere self. He can be passionate and cool, grave and light; he is always honest." Cezanne was always direct and agonizingly moral. 'Frankness of his means' coupled with his dedicated search of the pure form took him to a pedestal which is reserved for the epoch-makers.

Robert Hughes has written "it may be that Cezanne was reaching for a kind of expression in painting that did not exist in his time and still does not in ours." His desperation for expression and 'sensitive spirit' was looking for a new sensibility. Despite the ripeness of his output that search remained unfulfilled. This unfulfilled search for a new sensibility is what makes him 'Patriarch of Modernism'. His sensibility was beyond his facility as bemoaned in his last letter to his son while describing the pain of realizing the sensations. He kept his agony from turning self destructive and that allowed him to practice his craft at a level which was heroic enough to open the floodgates of modern art. True modernism is a search, not a point, in art history. The fact that Cezanne remained unfulfilled is a testimony of his humanity and his greatness.

Edvard Munch: Illustrator of Maladies

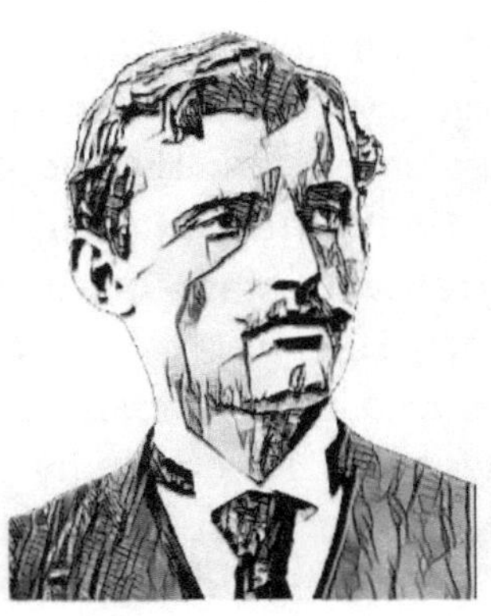

Much of the drama, depth and dance of Edvard Munch's artistic output is because of the sweet spot that he inhabits at the cusp of art, cinema and photography. He was deeply grounded in lyricism of painting and sufficiently interested in the modern inventions of his time to create an eclectic idiom that could take the best bits of the both the world. He painted cinema and photographs and he was an illustrator of many sensibilities and theories that were emerging at that time. Illustrators don't occupy the high pedestal in the pantheon of modern art. Photographs and cinemas are also treated as inadequate to address the exalted cravings of an artist who picks up brush to deal with his or her creativity. Not so with Edvard Munch. His perspective tricks, borrowed heavily from cinema, lent him the urgency needed to sharp-focus the anxious core of his work. His photograph-like depiction- 'Death in Sick Room' is a case in point, portrait of a stage or cinema screen ('Dance of Life' and 'Ashes') never degenerate into the lifelessness of camera output. He said "Photography will never compete with painting so long as the camera cannot be used in heaven or in hell." Edvard Munch took it upon himself to take the device in heaven and hell, mostly in hell. With all his modern tools and sensibilities he was ultimately an illustrator of maladies.

Dance of Life

Peter Schjeldahl from New Yorker Magazine gets it correct when he writes "His strongest works, dating from about 1890 to the early years of the last century, exalted pictorial functions—narrative and illustration—that were being combed out of modern painting as specialties more proper to literature and the popular arts." This was aided and reinforced by his 'ardent theatricality'. He was influenced by 'French painting (Gauguin and Van Gogh), Scandinavian theatre (Ibsen and Strindberg), and German philosophy (Nietzsche)'. Furthermore, he was bound to be aware of the developments that were taking place in the field of psycho-analysis. These influences provided a rich source for his dark repertoire. He was clued into the deepest anxieties of his times as interpreted by the leading theories of his times. He had artistic wherewithal and imagination to bring them on canvas with stark directness. He was at his best when his canvas was a narrative which is something more than just depiction. One can get more out of his paintings if one sees at least some of them as a screen shot or a moment on the stage. However, camera or stage angle should be taken only as entry points as Munch with his 'radically impure' style goes on chiselling newer realities of his themes making them truly timeless. "His disdain for normal technique and finish, his love of long, somewhat slurpy brush strokes that were more stained than painted, made all the difference. They enable him to give a new voice to the rawest emotions, to be dramatic without sentimentality, and to fuse process, subject and content" wrote another critic. His artistic eye made him keep on paring the details till the vision is distilled to the emotional core of the issue. He used the perspective given by the vocabulary of cinema and photography but gave his characters intense inner life. It is the amalgamation of direct representation of camera and radical impurity of a supreme artist that creates a melange of raw emotions that transcends limits both camera and canvas impose.

Death in Sickroom

Edvard Munch was born in Norway in 1863, the son of an Army surgeon whose family was stalked by death and illness. When he was 5, his mother died of tuberculosis; nine years later, his sister Sophie succumbed to the disease, giving him potent memories for his Sick Room paintings. Another sister was institutionalized for insanity. Munch committed himself several times for treatment of alcoholism and depression and underwent electric shock therapy. Although he had drawn since childhood, he entered college in Kristiania (as Oslo was called until 1925) to study engineering. Soon after, he transferred to art school and became involved with the Kristiania Bohemians. Munch had a difficult relationship with his father who was severe in his religious beliefs. He had an affair with Millie Thaulow, the wife of his teacher, patron and distant cousin Frits Thaulow. The affair ended badly but gave him raw material for many angst ridden paintings such as Ashes, Vampire. In 1885 Munch went to Paris and in 1889 enrolled in art school there. For the next two decades he spent most of every year in Germany, with summer trips to France and Scandinavia. He lived a long life and was active till the end that came in 1944.

Apart from the collision of emerging science with primal art, the jarring rush of Munch's art comes from other intersections. Robert Hughes has pointed out that Sigmund Freud's notion that self is the product of a battle between insatiable desires and unyielding social structures has found expression in Munch. Similarly he also explored the 'junction between objective and subjective.' All this resulted in a fertile arena where 'personal achieves the velocity of the universal.' It is this capacity of turning personal into universal that made a critic write that the source of Munch's longevity is to 'do with his extraordinary gift for coining both archetypes and shapes.' The thrust of his art 'took in such existential matters as birth, love, loss, emotional turmoil, the search for one's identity and the inevitable decline into death. In these paintings Munch struggled to render his own emotional and psychological traumas, including the deaths of his mother and older sister, as well as his doomed first real love affair, into universal images that resonated with the outside world'. By so doing, he said, he hoped to "understand the meaning of life" and to help others gain similar insights.``

In this he was helped by his 'self abnegating submission to the emotional truth'. Often his narratives border on melodrama, hence the talk of his 'ardent theatricality.' There is an element of hyperbole in painting. His self portrait 'On operation table' is filled with exaggerated details- A nurse is holding a bowl filled with blood and a blood stain is expanding on the sheet. Similarly 'Scream' is nothing if not an exaggerated expression of horror, anxiety or some kind of primal fear. He has been called an 'exuberant miserabilist' who indulges in 'exaggeration in service of truth'. "He has no shame when it comes to self-pity, hypochondria, jealousy or grief, and is never too proud to confess to lust or depression. He is the friend who doesn't censor the story as the rest of us might, and has no pretension of resignation or serenity or forgiveness. His emotions are open and energetically direct. His art is frankly invigorating" wrote Laura Cumming in Guardian.

In being such a successful illustrator of human maladies, Edvard Munch prepared the ground for anxious sensibilities to be aesthetically pleasing. He taught the generations how to appreciate the beauty of loneliness, melancholia, rejection or other such afflictions. By making them alive on canvas he created an idiom of pain that captured the universal appeal of a highly individual artist.

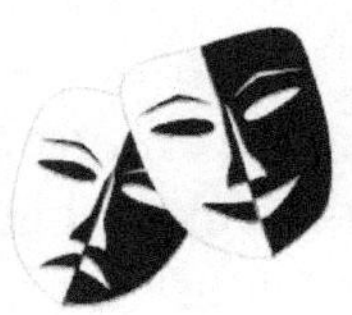

Toulouse Lautrec: Harem's Eunuch Who Went Wild

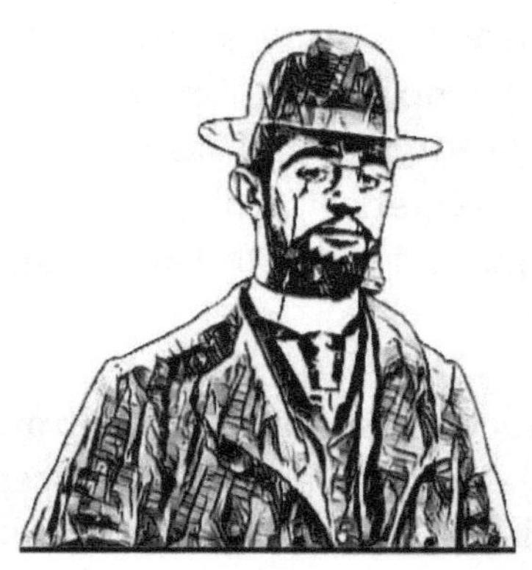

Toulouse Lautrec was philandering, absinthe drenched midget (his legs never grew to full length). He was also the most daring artist of his times- a period known as Belle Epoque - the beautiful period. To understand him fully we need to accept that he was a marketing genius fully in tune with the canons of rebranding. He took a seedy suburb and an experimental pleasure spot with questionable repute and transformed it into a upper middle class haunt for revelry complete with elusive combination of cultural sophistication and high sex appeal. He lent the high kicking women dancing

Cancan, brothels and general atmosphere of licentiousness of Montmartre in general and Moulin Rouge in particular with a degree of elegance. His genius lies in the fact that he kept the tart quotient intact while dangerously flirting with the menace of respectability.

No doubt Toulouse Lautrec is the foremost chronicler of the epoch in question- 1890s and thereabout. Paris, for good or worse, was imagined as the Mecca of hedonism and intellectual vibrancy. However this was not a simple reading of the 'movable feast' that Paris was. Anti-establishment feeling was strong but establishment was no slouch either.   Highbrow was revered but with a twist- a bit like 'offering of a bottle of scotch on the church altar'. The 'high culture' was willing and itching to "be dragged through the gutter." The hordes of young talented artists were leaving studio to capture life on the street.   Little wonder, the allure of Moulin Rouge and other guilty pleasures of Montmartre proved to be a big draw. The scene was not straight forward and Toulouse Lautrec wielded a crooked brush.

It is fashionable to discount his unusual physical appearance. However, things like these are hard to discount. One can only wonder that an aristocrat who was not even four and half feet tall would have got the kind of access that afforded Lautrec the 'immediacy of perspective.' He could adopt the role of the fly on the wall without disturbing the most intimate moments of his subjects. This backstage access owed a lot to his freakish appearance. He was the Harem's eunuch who went wild.

A fall out of this equation was his depiction of women as independent and individual entities. This was not very common even in Paris of those days. "He does not turn women into stereotypical sex objects, as does, say, Renoir. But neither is he clinically detached like Degas, who was a hugely important influence on Lautrec. Nor does he exoticize women à la Gauguin, or worship them as preternaturally beautiful goddesses, as the academic Bouguereau does." He is known for pictures of women like Jane Avril and Yvette Guilbert "who, on the stage anyway, are in charge of their own destinies. But he is good with ordinary women, too, and though they may be frumpy, gawky and otherwise less than beautiful, he always seems to like them."

He was born in 1864 into an aristocratic family that could trace its ancestry to the Crusades. Inbreeding which was common to such exalted lineage probably caused the congenital disease that turned him into a dwarfish, misshapen figure. The alcoholism and other illnesses that hastened his death at the age of 36 were byproducts of a career spent largely among the prostitutes, nightclub performers and hangers-on in the seamier quarters of Belle Epoque Paris.

Critic Robert Hughes has written "If the stream of life is subdivided into an infinity of fleeting moments, as it is by a culture based on photography, each looks like an actor's gesture, a pose—or a snapshot. This disarticulation was what Lautrec attempted, and one still marvels at the speed and accuracy of his notation, whether it was real (in his sketch pads) or feigned (in the finished theatrical lithographs)." Hughes here is catching the masterly quality of an artist who had imposed a studied distance between him and his subjects. He further elaborates "There was nothing expressionistic about

Lautrec. He did not revel in the miseries of the soul, and even his most pathetic images come to us across a measured distance and through a focused sense of human absurdity." The learned critic is very precise in his assessment of the master "one's admiration for Lautrec's craft, for the eggshell delicacy of spattered lithographic ink or the exact placement of a complementary color, ... it lasts just long enough to give a sense of wholly different organization—that the painting or the drawing is based on a precarious, swift sense of the real, exact but friable."

As an artist he works due to his flourish. He is a player who is good at handling high speed and volatile concepts. He thrives on turbulence and contains it with flair without losing on panache. Safety of caution is not for him and he does not fail in his wild experiments.

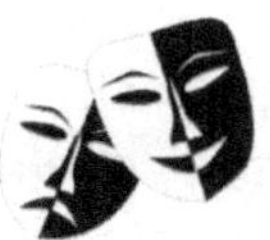

Lucien Freud: The Bohemian Monk and His Mounds of Feelings

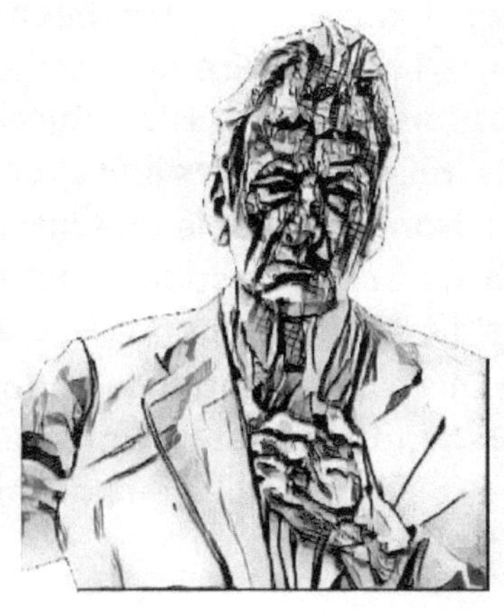

Lucien Freud was a painfully niche artist. He was a realist portrait painter- perhaps the best in modern times. His realism is unwavering and is a defining feature of his artistic output. Realism and portrait painting are the two anathemas of the modern day art world. Advent of photography must have played on Freud's mind when he made the genre of portrait painting his own. He set out to define realism for a realist and even a cursory look at his oeuvre is sufficient to highlight the deficiencies of photo-realism. He made human skin his arena and his weapon of choice was colour- loads of thick throbbing pigments creating fascinating mounds of feeling. If photography was ever a concern, it was not the picture postcard variety; it may well have been the family album. Lucien Freud never painted professional models. His subjects were his friends, relatives, wives and even daughters. "I work from the people that interest me and that I care about, in rooms that I live in and know," he is quoted in the New York Times. From this somewhat incestuous world of indoors and intimates emerged 'easy to admire, difficult to like' art of this grandson of Sigmund Freud.

Arena of skin

He never called his figurative paintings 'nudes' he called them naked portraits. When painting people without any clothes, he was dealing with the whole ethos and feeling ecosystem of nakedness. He was 'normally' miles away from sensuality when painting these nudes. His sitters were generally the people he knew, his friends, assistant, daughters and sons. He did not capture them in any airbrushed digestible form that glorifies the human body- a tradition that goes a long way back to masters of the classical period or even to primal cave paintings with exaggerated organs. In Lucien Freud's paintings 'decorum of nudity' is given a rude go by. His subjects don't convey the splendor of the human body or the sensuality of nudity. Here he conveys the everydayness of nudity which is very discomforting to the artistic eyes trained on the classical tradition of glorified nudes. He is almost clinical in getting the correct hue of human skin. He was liberal in applying paint-his principal weapon and painstaking in coercing the paint to come out with the spirit of the nakedness of the subject. It is a nakedness that is stark in its completeness, poignant in its vulnerability, almost repulsive in its details. He is neither photographic nor pornographic. Dead verisimilitude of the photographs and cheap and easy tantalization of pornographic are the last sensations that come to the mind of the viewers. He creates feelings that are dreary, heavy and above all true about humanity and its vulnerability. Robert Hughes wrote "in his own way Freud has done what Velazquez did: assimilate the life of the subject to the life of the paint surface and of each gesture held in it. Very few painters can do this. It is not a trick. This is the difference between painting something and merely rendering it -- between Freud's fat woman, which is radical art of the highest intensity, and, say, Fernando Botero's fat women, which are boring essays in the pneumatics of style."

He was not being sadistic or cruel to his subject when he painted them in such unflattering details. In fact, to a discerning eye it will appear a work of sympathy and attachment. Here, his insistence of avoiding professional models comes in. He was intimate with his subjects as lover, friend or father. This intimacy excluded domination and exploitation. In fact, many of his subjects, including his daughters who posed nude for him- have found the arduous experience of sitting- that was normally long stretching to months and sometimes years and physically exacting- the best way of bonding with the artist. His extraordinarily remarkable personality often made these bonding an experience to cherish.

The Old School Bohemian

Lucien Freud came from an impeccable pedigree. Lucian Michael Freud was born in Berlin on Dec. 8, 1922, and grew up in prosperous circumstances. His father, Ernst L. Freud, an architect, was Sigmund Freud's youngest son. His mother Lucie Brasch, who was painted by him after his father's death, was the heiress to a timber fortune. In 1933, after Hitler came to power, the Freuds moved to London. He was not a very promising student and was a difficult teenager. "In 1938, he was expelled from Bryanston, in Dorset, after dropping his trousers on a dare on a street in Bournemouth. But his sandstone sculpture of a horse earned him entry into the Central School of Arts and Crafts in London. He left there after a year to enroll in the East Anglian School of Drawing and Painting in Dedham.... In 1941, hoping to make his way to New York, Mr. Freud enlisted in the Merchant Navy, where he served on a convoy ship crossing the Atlantic. He got no nearer to New York than Halifax, Nova Scotia, and after returning to Liverpool developed tonsillitis and was given a medical discharge from the service."

His obituary in New York Times describes him as a bohemian of the old school who set up his studios in squalid neighborhoods, developed a 'Byronic reputation as a rake and gambled recklessly'. In 1948, he married Kitty Garman, the daughter of the sculptor Jacob Epstein. Kitty was the subject of many of his early important works like "Girl With Roses," "Girl With a Kitten" (1947) and "Girl With a White Dog" (1950-51). That marriage ended in divorce, as did his second marriage, to Lady Caroline Blackwood. He is survived by at least 14 acknowledged children from his first marriage and from a series of romantic relationships.

His early works were linear and thinly painted. Under the decisive influence of his friend Francis Bacon in the mid 50s, Freud abandoned this style and started moving "toward the brushy, searching portrait style of his mature work, with its severely muted palette of browns and yellows." This style kept on getting 'refined' into a more coarse and robust style complete with more voluminous application of paint and thicker brushes. Later, he had the luck of having a flush of late renaissance of talent. I will use the late Robert Hughes tribute to Freud here "Most artists, one imagines, dream of achieving a great late style -- the uprush and resolution in old age, careless of aesthetic risk, sometimes even a little mad, that carry a life's effort into profundity. Few, obviously, manage anything of the sort. The retrospective of paintings by Lucian Freud, 71 (at that time), which opened last week at New York City's Metropolitan Museum of Art, sets before us one who has." This rush continued till very last when he died in July 2011 at 88.

Creating art without artifice

Freud's paintings often flirt with the danger of falling in the caricature trap. Heightened realism can get cartoonish and Freud in his time engaged with obvious caricatures (no I am not talking of the queen of England whom he painted). He shared with Salvador Dali the penchant of realism and love for details but he rejected Surrealism after initial forays into it. "The Painter's Room" (1943) has strong Surrealistic traits. He was totally divorced from the weird imagination that was the mainstay of Surrealism. "I could never put anything into a picture that wasn't actually there in front of me," he is quoted to tell Robert Hughes. "That would be a pointless lie, a mere bit of artfulness." This is an astounding achievement that he survived caricature trap despite hyper reality and, may be more importantly, created art while abhorring artfulness

Artifice is what makes art differ from documentary reality. As poetry is art of 'sweet excesses' art also needs sweet excess. Freud achieved the near impossible task of getting this excess by being fanatically rooted in reality. He captured the everydayness of his subjects. Anything more would fall in the ambit of 'mere bit of artfulness'. The traction of artistic appeal is gained by the intensity of his feeling of getting to the soul of reality. He keeps on chiseling with his hog hair brush till the reality comes out. This process made his pursuit of fidelity transcend mere similarity and art was born.

This load of intensity kept him away from Non European, particularly, American fame. He wasn't modern enough as he was a realist portrait artist and Warhol-infused America was not fine-tuned enough for his dreary realistic works. It later changed. He gained respect of the New World and was made very rich too by insane demand for his paintings among the well heeled connoisseurs.

He created art by obsessing with his subject. He was brutally slow (though his vast output may indicate otherwise). He was a monk in his studio. He was doggedly unsentimental and unwavering in teasing the soul out of his renderings without resorting to fireworks. He has come to be synonymous with intense art of high calibre and epithet of 'greatest realist painter of modern times' has stuck.

Robert Hughes- The consummate curmudgeon

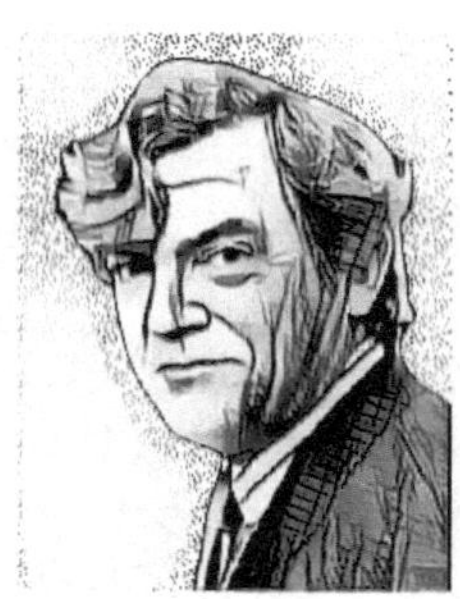

He always had the right words to describe it and his explanation always seemed complete. It was this knack of zooming in to the crux of the appeal of an artwork that made Robert Hughes the formidable force in the world of art-criticism. His charisma was rooted in uber intellectualism nurtured by encyclopedic knowledge and tempered by street fighter brawn. He was very literate and very contentious. True to his profession he had strong opinions and enough ammunition to defend those opinions against anyone.

Many of his obituaries have conveyed the impression that he did not realize his full potential. There was an undercurrent there that may be due to his involvement with media juggernaut, he could not contribute in a more enduring way. In the encomiums, there was a struggle to convey what he stood for. On the other hand, there were mentions of the criticism that he was seen as a reactionary critic who failed to fully appreciate the later day developments. In an otherwise glowing tribute Benjamin Genocchio wrote in the New York Times "I am not going to venture any views on his critical opinions of art and artists, most of which were shaped in the early 1960s and which, by the 1990s, increasingly seemed out of touch with developments in contemporary art. He found little to like, turning into a kind of reactionary crank." Not that he was being criticized- far from it; his death last month brought a surge of undiluted admiration from his fraternity. These negative strands spoken with a combative camaraderie of critics which is not supposed to be dimmed by the funeral shadow, do need rebuttal as Robert Hughes is not just famous but he is important too. His contribution should not come under shadow because of the arc lights that he courted with such bruising intensity.

Enduring Appeal

Question of the lasting importance of Hughes often comes from the very narrow interpretation of the notion of importance. Many feel that Hughes could have given a theory or a framework of art appreciation. There is a nagging impression that in the ephemeral world of media he failed to contribute in a durable way. More than anything else many of his admirers fail to identify him with any particular type of art. Hughes was not an academician. Notwithstanding his erudition and vast knowledge, he wasn't a pedant. He has created enduring and academically sound work in the form of books and monographs but they only partially define his contribution. He has written definitive treatises on world's most important cities, art and artists. He has given a true classic in 'Fatal Shores' an account of settling of Australia. On account of these only, he is an enduring intellectual figure in the fields of history and art. However he is important from a far deeper perspective. Academic tomes are needed and have a place and Hughes has a first rate academic oeuvre. But beyond the ivory towers of academia, art criticism has a very public purpose - that of identifying, analyzing, and most importantly refining public taste.

Arbiter of Public Taste

Art critic is not just doing the analysis of present trends but also carries the burden of making art accessible to the public. In him or her resides the custodian of the aesthetic heritage of mankind. He is able to tell western public what does it mean to be a Hon'ami Koetsu in 16th century Japan or what made Reubens what he was or what torturous demons propelled Goya or Van Gogh. Does there exist, if at all, any redeeming feature in Warhol.

The critic is the arbiter of public taste, its aggregator and its disseminator. He sits on judgement about the public sensibilities and in turn forms them. Many artists need such interpreters to convey their appeal and Robert Hughes had this knack of spotting greatness and intellectual and communicative wherewithal to make this greatness mainstream. He interpreted Lucian Freud for the US public. He declared Freud to be the greatest realist painter alive (at that time) and said "... the extraordinary flavor of the nudes and portraits by Lucien Freud, the 52-year-old grandson of Sigmund: more psychic territory is crossed in Freud's scrutiny of a few square inches of worn flesh than one might find in a whole roomful of recent American realism"- America agreed. Lucian Freud will be Freud without Hughes also but with him he is accessible to a larger chunk of humanity and with far deeper intensity- the pleasure increases many times over. The point here is that art needs public arbiters equally or, maybe, more than the academic pronouncements. From this perspective, Robert Hughes is a figure of historical importance.

It is a bit of a surprise that there is very little clarity about what he stood for. He was nothing if not opinionated. It was his trade to have an opinion and clear cut biases. He liked, and liked strongly, Lucian Freud, Picasso, Matisse, Cézanne, and other modern masters. He absolutely adores Goya. He was pretty clear that art is about imagination, colour scheme, symmetry of execution and draftsmanship. He liked his art to break new grounds but for him art was about aesthetics and feeling. It had to conform to the basic minimum of aesthetic inventiveness or even 'beauty'. After watching the Matisse exhibition he wrote "Such is our fin-de-siecle. On every side, the idea of quality is ritually attacked, so that many young artists have come to doubt the most basic experience involved in comparing one artwork with another -- namely, that there are differences of intensity, articulateness, radiance, between works of art; that some speak more convincingly than others; and that this is not a political matter." It was on the grounds of 'intensity, articulateness, radiance' he did not like much "wretchedly stylish woods of an already decayed, pulped-out postmodernism." He was brutal when he found that something that is not 'art' for him is being touted as one. One such unfortunate soul was Basquiat, graffiti painter who died in 1988 of a heroin overdose, Hughes' 'tribute' ran under the headline, "Requiem for a Featherweight." Basquiat, he wrote, was "a small, untrained talent caught in the buzz saw of art world promotion, absurdly overrated by dealers, collectors, and no doubt to their future embarrassment, by critics." He really disliked the crass commercialization of the art world. This often propped him up for the attack as a reactionary or a conservative who was not in tune with the new developments.

Master of Put-down

It is true that his first instinct towards the new trends of installation art and extreme experiments in public tastes was that of anger and contempt. However, he always argued cogently for his contempt and was brutal with his putdown. New York Times quotes him describing the work of Jeff Koons as "so overexposed that it loses nothing in reproduction and gains nothing in the original." However, he is not averse to inventiveness. He is not very enthusiastic about Warhol but he recognizes his genius. In fact his evaluation of Warhol puts the artists in proper perspective. He writes "His (Warhol's)contribution was the image taken from advertising or tabloid journalism: grainy, immediate, a slice of unexplained life half-registered over and over, full of slippages and visual stutters. Marilyn Monroe repeated 50 times, 200 Campbell's soup cans, a canvas filled edge to edge with effigies of Liz, Jackie, dollar bills or Elvis. Absurd though these pictures looked at first, Warhol's fixation on repetition and glut emerged as the most powerful statement ever made by an American artist on the subject of a consumer economy. The cranking out of designed objects of desire was so faithfully mirrored in Warhol's images and so approvingly mimicked in his sense of culture that no one, in fact, could be sure what he thought." This makes it clear that Warhol was about presentation rather than representation. While acknowledging the value of Warhol he is very clear "Warhol's early works were the ones that mattered. He began as a commercial artist, became for a time (between about 1962 and 1968) a fine artist with something akin to genius and then lapsed back into a barely disguised form of commercial art."

He is acidic about the rampant commercialization. This sharpness of opinion may have contributed to his image as an out of sync curmudgeon. However, this may be noted he had a fine eye, howsoever conservative, which was always open to the value of art.

Nothing demonstrates his opinionated self than the description in his New York Time obituary- "About artists he admired, like Lucian Freud, he cast the stakes in nothing less than heroic terms. "Every inch of the surface has to be won," he wrote of Freud's canvases in The Guardian in 2004, "must be argued through, bears the traces of curiosity and inquisition — above all, takes nothing for granted and demands active engagement from the viewer as its right." ...."Nothing of this kind happens with Warhol, or Gilbert and George, or any of the other image-scavengers and recyclers who infest the wretchedly stylish woods of an already decayed, pulped-out postmodernism."

He is arguably the most successful art evangelist in the television era. His forthright manner, his conviction and confrontationist personality shone on the screen. "The Shock of the New," his eight-part documentary about the development of modernism from the Impressionists through Warhol, was seen by more than 25 million viewers when it ran first on BBC and then on PBS and the book that he spun off from it was a "stunning critical performance" and hugely popular.

To conclude-

His comments on the two of the greatest artists are the best way to demonstrate how he made high art accessible to us without pandering to the lowest common denominator.

On Picasso- "In his work, everything is staked on sensation and desire. His aim was not to argue coherence but to go for the strongest level of feeling. He conveyed it with tremendous plastic force, making you feel the weight of forms and the tension of their relationships mainly by drawing and tonal structure. He was never a great colorist, like Matisse or Pierre Bonnard. But through metaphor, he crammed layers of meaning together to produce flashes of revelation. In the process, he reversed one of the currents of modern art. Modernism had rejected storytelling: what mattered was formal relationships. But Picasso brought it back in a disguised form, as a psychic narrative, told through metaphors, puns and equivalences. The most powerful element in the story--at least after Cubism-- was sex."

On Matisse- "In its thoughtfulness, steady development, benign lucidity, and wide range of historical sources, Matisse's work utterly refutes the notion that the great discoveries of modernism were made by violently rejecting the past. His work was grounded in tradition - and in a much less restless and ironic approach to it than Picasso's."...... "His studio was a world within the world: a place of equilibrium that, for sixty continuous years, produced images of comfort, refuge, and balanced satisfaction. Nowhere in Matisse's work does one feel a trace of the alienation and conflict which modernism, the mirror of our century, has so often reflected."

Andy Warhol: String of Banalities as High Art

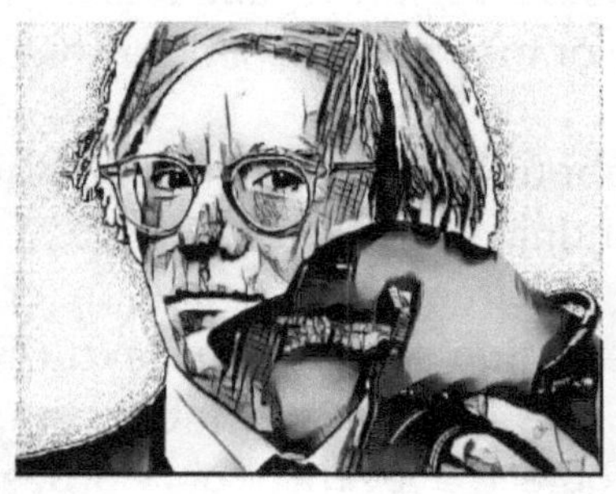

The moment you start ascribing meaning to a can of soup, you miss the entire point of Andy Warhol's art. Suffixing Warhol's work with the label of art has its issues. Art normally involves an element of sensual/sensory pleasure. A premise of expression or representation is inherent. But the soup can in question is just that- a soup can- not an act of subversion or deeply nuanced meaning. If he was subverting anything it was the time honoured tradition of high art. Warhol was not seeking an escape from the harshness of reality but accepting that as the arena of once being. He was not representing or conveying the inherent meaning of his subjects. He was only labelling them or putting them in a frame. He was foregrounding the obvious. To use his words, it was "about liking things." You may or may not like him for that.

He was about 'presenting' things rather than 'representing' things. This allowed him to be free of requirements of unique creation. 'Representation' entails an exclusivity of output. It is the artist's interpretation of some object, event or process. A representation of female form will find expression in cubist reconstruction of Dora Maar in Picasso's work or Odalisques of Matisse or sturdy physicality of Hussain's nudes. These are customized creations which abhor mass production. Even portraits like Mona Lisa are not free of enigmatic intimacy of exclusive creation. But in the Warholian universe even serigraph prints using silk screen technique is valid art because he is not representing but presenting. His Marilyn Monroe series along with Cow wallpaper, Liz, Elvis, Accidents, Chairman Mao and Michael Jackson series were mass production and high art at the same time. Marrying this breach was a monumental achievement and Warhol did it in style. Distinction between the traditional art and his art is illustrated by his failure in the case of Mona Lisa where he tried his reproduction mania in serigraph prints of multiple Mona Lisas called 'Thirty are Better Than One.' It looked strained and populist in a bad sense. It lacked the aesthetic sensations of his Marilyn or Elvis and a major part of that was the representative appeal that makes Mona Lisa an icon that it is. However, somehow his fetish for the obvious was not devoid of beauty.

Formal decor and chromatic panache of his output is timeless and is hip even today, almost half a century later. Following one of his idols Matisse, Warhol "redid the world's palette in tart" a new colour scheme emerged after 1962, the year when he blasted into the artistic consciousness of the world. He imparted lesser explored hues like citron, burnt orange, apple green and cobalt blue to the lexicon of cool. He managed to bring the kitsch and posh disarmingly close and his main achievement was that he made it all seem irritatingly valid. He achieved this by combining aesthetic sophistication with the reproducibility of the mass production.

This success at combining classical core, if not the form of high art, with the vernacular psyche gave him a stature to use his intuitive éclat regarding formal beauty and very hip colour consciousness to define a new chic. As the trends go, this Warhol impact has endured surprisingly long. If his blandness of devotion to the obvious made him so pervasive that his influence or presence is very difficult to deny. His rich sense of colour, which made him such a successful commercial artist in the first place, keeps him ubiquitous. Right from the bottle of Absolut Vodka to the neon induced glitz of Time Square or Tokyo to illustrated children books, he is everywhere. His motifs can be seen on clothes of top fashion houses, on shoes, watches, logos advertisements. No doubt his is a defining presence on the artistic landscape of the later part of the century gone by.

Robert Hughes of Time Magazine has called Warhol's fame his most authoritative creation- "the meticulous construction of a persona vivid in its coy blandness, pervasive and teasing in its appeal to the media, and deathlessly inorganic." This makeover of the son of an immigrant Czech coal miner named

Warhola in Pittsburgh, to Warhol was in line with his philosophy of 'absoluteness of systematic banality'. In his decline- a phase after he was shot by one of his hanger ons in 1968, he was more famous for being Andy Warhol than his work. In this phase he was prolific and active but as one critic has put it 'intensity leaked out of his works'. A trashy melodrama overtook what was the genuine exhilaration of discovering something new. When surprise waned, his work stopped giving the same degree of aesthetic sensation. Detachment which provided a new standing to his work started appearing forced. But even in his decline he was interesting and provocative. Chairman Mao series bears testimony to it.

He had an uncanny knack of grasping the 'ripeness of the moment'. His was a life of celebrity acutely tuned to the pulse of media space. This ability along with the ability to grasp an image and instilling it with 'visual clout' put him at the centre of the orgy of fame and kept him there for a long time. Originator of the phrase '15 minutes of fame' had a longer moment in the spotlight- a moment that still lingers.

Andy Warhol: A Hotel Notebook Summation

Antithesis of traditional notion of an artist Warhol was not about passion, angst or some sort of catharsis of sufferings. In fact, art is not 'actually' about all that. We just like our artists that way. Art like poetry is about 'sweet excesses'. It is about aesthetic sensations. Artists have been purveyors of condensed sensations of all sorts which could very broadly be categorized as aesthetic. If history of art has proved anything, it is the multiplicity of sources, contexts or even paradigms of such sensations. Being orthodox about one's fix of artistic rush may be a matter of personal choice. However, on a general level, excluding anything out of it is ignorance at best and totalitarian at worst. Warhol was producing aesthetic sensations in a sufficient number of people. More and more artists were being emboldened to look for alternate sources to create aesthetic sensations. His own take on the dynamics of art was to foreground the mundane or obvious. He placed a frame to Coke bottle and it started impacting aesthetically. He was serious about liking things and succeeded in communicating that.

He was about 'presenting' things rather than 'representing' things. He tested this notion and felt vindicated by the raw irritation created by his output. He was perceptive enough to realize the aesthetic stirrings that his Campbell Soup series or Brillo Boxes created in the artistic circles. And that liberated him. Once, on sure footing about his raw material (anything goes), he moved to Films and silk screen paintings. He produced films of static shots of the Empire State building and people sleeping. These were long movies of 8-20 hour duration, where nothing much was happening. He was just pointing to an object long enough, allowing the innate neural aesthetic coding to do its work. His 'screen tests' where he asked his subjects to sit and just stare at the camera were also in the same vein. Intellectuals like Susan Santog and Bob Dylan subjected themselves to this fishbowl treatment. "His better paintings, in which pure aesthetic sensation transcends subject matter, are too particular to be taken as specimens of anything other than themselves" said The New Yorker.

Condensed Sensations: Art of Henri Matisse

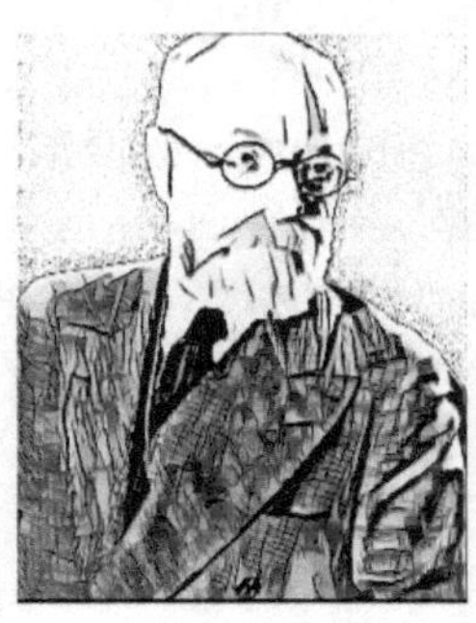

"Whosoever does not have a low opinion of joy is a likely connoisseur of Matisse's Art."

Henri Matisse defies slotting. He emerged on the art scene of the early 20th century as 'fauve' – the wild beast- demolishing every rule of formality and use of colour yet his grounding in tradition is beyond doubt. He never painted or signed a political resolution. Epoch-making world wars, violent ideological struggles, Nazism,

Fascism, nuclear arsenal have no trace in his work but he claims that 'painting is life by other means'. His is the most soothing and colourful repertoire but in it are the most drastic experimentations in the history of art. He has been derided as 'beautiful', 'interior designer' even as suffering from 'mental illness' for his art. At the same time in his lifetime and later he remains a 'paladin of modernism'. It may sound fanatic but we may safely agree that whosoever does not have a low opinion of joy is a likely connoisseur of Matisse's Art.

Socio-political prism is a wrong parameter to apply to Matisse. He is undoubtedly a painter of luxury, comfort and refuge. His aesthetic sensibilities are more inclined towards pleasantness. His oeuvre exudes calm and luxuriant beauty. However, from this universe of balance and pastoral bliss, his relentless confrontation with the rules of the game comes shining through. His instinctive grasp of the form and emotions surrounding his subjects along with his natural talent for visual communication enabled him to create high art out of seemingly trivial and occasionally childlike output. He once remarked 'one must study an object for a long time to know what its sign is.' He was able to catch the sign with its innermost depth and communicate it in terms of forms and colours which were entirely his own. One of his most famous paintings 'The Dance' (1910) is the case in point. Dubbed as 'one of the few wholly convincing images of physical ecstasy made in the twentieth century' the painting captures the rapture and energy with very simple anatomical details of five dancers 'deliberately gauche and childish'. Saturated blues and greens of painting along with terracotta flesh do their mysterious alchemy to give us the complete and fully realized product where his sublime reading of the sign ties flawlessly to the basic physical details. Result is a painting 'modernist in a way that has not faded.'

Matisse could say 'Exactitude is not truth' and prove it by conveying emotions and 'the inherent' truth of human situations. His Conversation (1910) shows the painter in his pajamas having conversation with Mme. Matisse. This very basic rendition looks unskilled but somehow manages to impress as a masterpiece evoking a complex interplay of sight and imagination. Great art has that liberty.

A logical corollary of 'the quest for depicting the inherent truth' was capturing the core by chiselling out the surplus from the ultimate form. Starkly unequivocal form, devoid of any ambiguity was his quest. His achievement is in accomplishing that within the broad and pleasant ambit of decorative formality. In his work this minimalist approach never compromises the monumentality of the output. His painting like Blue Nude: Memory of Biskra (1907) was precursor to the ultimate distillation of form in his paper cut outs- the definitive chromatic and rhythmic improvisation. He said his life was 'a constant struggle for complete expression with a minimum of elements.' He achieved this in his cut outs with sculptural richness. His La Danseuse (1949) Nudes in cut outs especially Zulma (1950) exemplify an exhilarating economy of contours with maximum articulation. Not only with regard to formal distillation but they were also the pinnacle of his audacity of colour. These cutouts are testimony of his gift of creating beauty with any medium. It was a prolonged hurrah of an aging giant.

'Everything that is not useful in the picture is, it follows, harmful' he said in 1908, He fulfilled that in the evening of his life.

The 'modernist' was a creature of tradition. Influence of Courbet is evident in the greens of Large Landscape, Mont Alban of 1918. Manet whispers from the tantalizing ambience of Fish and Lemons, 1921. Distinctness of black as a colour in its own right, not just a darkness induced by the absence of colour, recalls the earlier master. Emergence of photography had rendered faithful recreation reality a less exalted pursuit. Impressionists started exploiting the formless sensations of art with disappearing laws of perspective. Gaugin, Van Gogh and Cezanne stretched the vistas of colour. They deepened the role of colour in communicating the mental state and emotions.

It was left to masters of 20th century Matisse and Picasso to take the process to a different level. They did it by making the act of painting the supreme end in itself. This was a liberating foundation as it allowed them to have a virgin template to work out their own rules. Their prodigious talent and gigantic genius made them a worthy bearer of the mantle of the prophets of new art. Picasso's phenomenal talent was directed at torturous reinterpretation of perspective. He was a protean giant shattering the form and imposing his will through his lines. Matisse called himself a 'slave of form' and was dedicated to convey it with purest economy of strokes. His primary vehicle was colour and lines were subservient to it. His were not abstract paintings but pure forms that conveyed luxury. Matisse's creative space has been called a 'boudoir' whereas Picasso's brutal intelligence made it an 'operating theatre'.

Matisse was a genius of colour. His chromatic panache is perhaps unsurpassed. Van Gough's yellow is there but Matisse took colour as the very condensation of emotions. Art critic Robert Hughes has wondered "what other artist could handle those deep, resonant cobalt blues, those fuchsias and oranges, those velvety blacks and soprano yellows, without producing an effect akin to coloured gumballs?" His intuitive grasp of colours was, like music, equated with nuances of feelings. His lines were not 'the container of his colour but the edge produced by its expansion.' He said that colours must react to one another to avoid a cacophony. To achieve this he professed, 'let colour be the force in a painting'. His infallible gift of creating hues, though at odds with nature, was able to produce the most 'right' experience. This he achieved through uncanny juxtaposition and inherently rebellious harmony. His 'The Red Studio' of 1911 can be seen in this context. A crimson drenched canvas, the painting is an aggressive testimonial of Matisse's use of colour as a vehicle to scream fictitiousness of art. An artificiality that is a potent device to convey the most deeply felt feeling with utmost force and precision. It is not an easy painting to watch as it does not allow you to enter from any one point but forces you to take a plunge. Objects do guide the eye but this is done not to give you a feel of the plasticity of the studio but the emotion that it perhaps induced in Matisse. No wonder 'The Red Studio' has been admired for proving that 'art can form its own republic of pleasure.'

'The fauve' was a law student who took up painting rather late and in his day-to-day life he maintained a formal profile with staid tweeds, professorial visage and fierce protection of his private life. However, He is all about passion and emotions. He sought condensation of sensations. Once ignited by the passion his pictorial intelligence was capable of taking him to any length on the path of greatness. He wrote in Notes of a Painter (1908) "I prefer, by insisting upon essential character, to risk losing charm in order to obtain greater stability. Underlying the succession of moments which constitutes the superficial existence of beings and things, and which is continually modifying and transforming them, one can search for a truer, more essential character, which the artist will seize so that he may give to reality a more lasting interpretation." He accomplished that but the bigger achievement is that he did so without compromising on beauty and formal decor. This is the core of his appeal.

Creative Predator: Picasso's Women and His Art

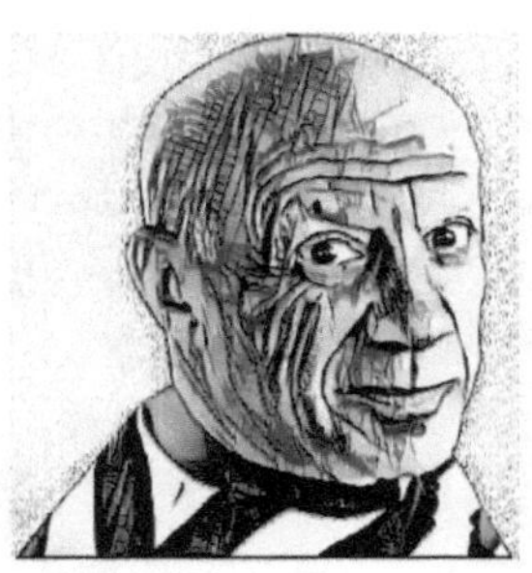

Most of Picasso's women could not recover from the intensity of their encounter with him. "When I die," Picasso had prophesied, "it will be a shipwreck, and as when a huge ship sinks, many people all around will be sucked down with it."

Picasso's defining influence on 20th century painting is evident from the impact his experimentation had on all areas of the art world. His monumental talent, absence of definite theory of art, continuous reinvention and very long life led in the fast lane of emotional upheavals have created myth replete with conquests both as an artist and as a seducer. His prolific output amply reflects the presence of countless women in his life as lovers, enchantresses, wives or simply art dealers. These are intense encounters, their portrayal is relentlessly real, unabashed and invariably creative. No wonder that one of the most expensive works of art in history is a Picasso. "Nude, Green Leaves and Bust", was sold to a telephone buyer at Christie's New York auction for $106.5m. The 1932 work was a portrait of Marie-Thérèse Walter, his mistress during one of his most creative phases.

Picasso's myth is basically a masculine saga of creativity. He had an amazing capacity to translate his feelings on the canvas. His execution of his vision was resolutely assured and quick. Succession of women was central to his life and his work. Earthy and sensuous Oliver, delicate Eva, his ballerina wife Olga, beautiful Marie-Thérèse, photographer Dora Maar, companion who 'survived Picasso' Françoise Gilot and his wife during the last three decades of his life - Jacqueline provided enduring themes to his painting and acted as a muse to trigger his talents.

Known as "la belle Fernande" Fernande Oliver was the artists' first real love and her presence is often credited with bringing out Picasso from the melancholy of 'Blue Period' to 'Rose Period'. She was his muse during the heady days of birth of Cubism and continued her reign till 1910 they broke up finally in 1912.

She stormed into Picasso's life on the afternoon of August, 04, 1904, when he blocked her way to a shelter where she was running to escape from an unexpected thunderstorm. Drenched to the skin she was offered a kitten, which was saved by Picasso from the storm. She could not escape his laughter and magnetic black eyes, he was besotted by her statuesque charms. She was four months older to Picasso and had a history of two failed major relationships. Gertrude Stein, Picasso's major buyer for a long time has written " For good or for bad, everything was natural in Fernande." She has been described as naturally beautiful, naturally intelligent, naturally creative, and naturally lazy. In the same naturally lazy way she naturally surrendered to the possessive passions of Picasso. It was an encounter of a worldly-wise woman and a creative genius whose sexual horizons were limited to traditional initiations in the local whorehouses. He took some time to adjust to the challenge of adult sexuality and an enduring relationship. He was a jealous lover and did not allow her to go out alone. She was satisfied in her Bohemian settings and her lethargy and unbridled sexuality suited Picasso's requirements admirably. Her exuberant beauty and robust figure had a positive impact. The vitality of companionship kept depression away from her pampered lover. Her memoir gives a glimpse of Picasso before he became the demigod of modern art. Due to her influence he achieved a level of maturity where "he could take delight in sadness without sympathising with it". She left Picasso for the Futurist painter - Ubaldo Oppi. Picasso, the master of regeneration, seduced Eva (Mercelle Humbert) from her Polish painter-lover within 24 hours. His devastation at the loss of first real love of life is evident from what he wrote to Braque, the co-founder of Cubism, "Fernande left yesterday with a Futurist painter... What will I do about the dog?"

Fernande's place was gradually taken over by Eva. Eva & Fernande were a study in contrast. Eva was a delicate being in need of protection, while Fernandes was a natural survivor. To demonstrate how precious Marcelle was to him, Picasso renamed her Eva.

Eva was deeply loved by Picasso but that did not stop him from flirting with Gaby Lespinasse a beautiful twenty-seven-year-old Parisian during hospitalisation of Eva and coming out with sensual paintings of naked Gaby. Eva's poor health proved fatal. On December 14 1915, Eva died. "My poor Eva is dead," he wrote to Gertrude Stein. "It was a great sorrow . . . she was always so good to me"

Picasso met Olga Khokhlova, his first wife when Jean Cocteau, the "frivolous prince" and Picasso's passport to high society, took him to design costumes and stage sets for Sergie Diaghilev's new ballet —Parade. Olga was one of sixty dancers in Diaghilev's troupe. Her restrained manners, traditional beauty coupled with a hint of nobility of descent caught Picasso's attention. Her normalcy was a positive attraction for

Picasso who had led a life of abnormal romantic encounters, a life which at the time was not proving to be a very happy one for him. Olga saw a safe prospect in the painter who was important enough for being given a substantial position in the production of Diaghilev. For Picasso it was an escape to "luxurious ordinariness". They got married on 12 July 1918, first at a civil ceremony then in an elaborate Russian Orthodox Church marriage. She ruled his paintings from 1917 to throughout 20's. In this period, neoclassical images were challenged by Cubist abstractions. During the beginning of their relationship, Olga's portraits were marked by tenderness and sacred esteem with which Picasso treated her. However, by the end of their marriage, these classically inspired portraits are gone. Now, Olga has a skull-like head with jaws; her image emerges from mechanical and animal forms as in 'Seated Bather' of 1930. A savage distortion of human form was all too evident. Olga marks a clear-cut break from the bohemian lifestyle of Picasso's previous incarnation and introduced him to the life of traditional respectability. Her lethargic but obsessive resolve to keep her marriage alive, could not stop Picasso from moving towards new relationships.

In 1927 he saw athletic blond, beautiful and almost thirty years younger than him- Marie-Thérèse. She wrote later " he simply grabbed me by the arm and said 'I am Picasso! You and I are going to do great things together....I resisted for six months but you don't resist Picasso. You have ......understood me, a woman does not resist Picasso." It was a great sexual odyssey unfettered by age, taboo and responsibility. Marie- Thérèse's appeal lay in her submissiveness and willingness to fulfill any whimsical or sadistic demand of Picasso. He used to see in her proof of his power and sexual magnetism. He experienced the thrill of a forbidden relationship as she was too young and he kept Olga in the dark about her existence. Marie-Thérèse, the secret companion, is depicted as soft, round and youthful. Her laughter appears unburdened and she exudes lightness of carefree spirit. Yet, years later, in the dusk of their relationship, she confessed that Picasso did not want her to laugh and was always telling her to "be serious." In his later works of the 1920s all of Picasso's visual references of Marie- Thérèse were veiled, a decade later it seems that he no longer wanted to be secretive about his new lover. It is through Marie-Thérèse's image we get the most explicit depiction of Picasso's sexuality, reflection of a boundary-less unrestrained relationship between the Master and his willing sexual and emotional slave. Her several portraits such as The Mirror (1932), Sleeping Nude (1932),Girl Before a Mirror (I932) and Nude Asleep in a Landscape (1934) allude to the highly passionate nature of their relationship.

In 1935 Olga left him, Marie-Thérèse gave birth to a girl and Picasso met Dora Maar. Dora Maar was a model, photographer and a reasonably talented painter herself. She was an intellectual companion who even co-produced a painting, signed 'Picamaar'. It was a period when he had a wife, a concubine and an official mistress. Dora photo-documented the creation of 'Guernica', Picasso's most celebrated painting and arguably the most potent anti-war piece of art ever created. There was reportedly one incident During the period when 'Guernica' was being painted, when Marie-Thérèse and Dora Maar came to blows while quarrelling over Picasso. All this time Picasso calmly went on creating his greatest statement against human conflict. It is said that Picasso enjoyed having power over people by setting them in competition with each other. By the time Second World War entered its second year Marie-Thérèse was reduced to an emotional pulp quivering in anticipation of Picasso's next dose of physical and emotional solace. Even Dora was brutalized. In his painting there was once again, a complete transformation of womanhood. He painted dog-faced portraits of Dora Maar while turning her into a servile animal in real life also.

In 1943 he met the woman who "survived Picasso " Françoise Gilot was young enough to be his granddaughter but she was a perfect match for the wiles of the monstrous sexual predator. Picasso's seduction of her was a game between two evenly matched players. An outwitted Picasso found himself loving a precocious young lady who had fallen in love with him with her eyes wide open. Dora Maar, smug in her intellectual superiority, refused to believe that she could be replaced by a new young thing in Picassso's life, "may be in bed but never on table" she once remarked. Very soon she was falling apart and developed a neurotic craving for regaining Picasso's attention. Whereas Picasso's relationship with Françoise fell into a pattern where he avoided her when she softened while ran after her when she neglected him. She left him twice to come back. She bore him two children. Françoise was intelligent and independent enough to want to escape from Picasso. Despite her emotional miseries she kept her talent alive and by the end of forties, a time came when she was being feted for her costume designs and other artistic works, while Picasso waited for her. She also had relationships with other men. Françoise Gilot's controversial 1964 book, 'My Life with Picasso' became a source of inspiration for several feminist writings on the artist's misogynist personality. Her relationship with the icon was the theme of the successful movie "Surviving Picasso" Academy Award winner Sir Anthony Hopkins played Picasso with remarkable verve and authenticity. In 1953 she finally left Picasso.

From 1954 onwards, begins "l'époque Jacqueline" Jacqueline was his second wife and final companion. It was after a season of violent artistic creations, loneliness and endless womanizing, in the wake of Françoise's desertion, Picasso allowed Jacqueline to realize her infinite devotion. She was fiercely protective of and fanatically devoted to Picasso, his health, his peace, his need to remain productive were supreme for her. Françoise Gilot had pointed out that Picasso's women started as goddesses and ended as doormats. Jacqueline reversed the process. Her association with Picasso was the longest among the main feminine influences in the master's life. Her patient nursing kept him productive till the ninety-second year of his life. Her longevity made her the most widely used model who was explored more deeply than perhaps any model in the history of art. It is her vulnerability that gives a new intensity to the combination of cruelty and tenderness that endows Picasso's paintings of women with their pathos and their strength. The dedications on the countless drawings reveal that Picasso became more and more besotted as he became more and more reliant on Jacqueline. She developed the most varied skills, acting in turn as secretary, interpreter, agent, cook, poet, driver, nurse, photographer, model, and trouble-shooter. She gave Picasso his space and kept herself busy with other things while he worked. Her contribution is evident from the last coherent words of a dying Picasso to his doctor, he said "You are wrong not to be married. It is useful".

Most of his women could not recover from the intensity of their encounter with Picasso. "When I die," Picasso had prophesied, "it will be a shipwreck, and as when a huge ship sinks, many people all around will be sucked down with it." On October 20, 1977, in the year of the fiftieth anniversary of their meeting, Marie-Thérèse hanged herself in the garage of her house in Juan-les-Pins. "She couldn't bear the thought of him alone, his grave surrounded by people who could not possibly give him what she had given him."

Just after midnight on October 15, 1986, Jacqueline shot herself in the temple. She had left behind a list of everyone she wanted at her funeral.

Salvador Dali: Realism for the Unreal World

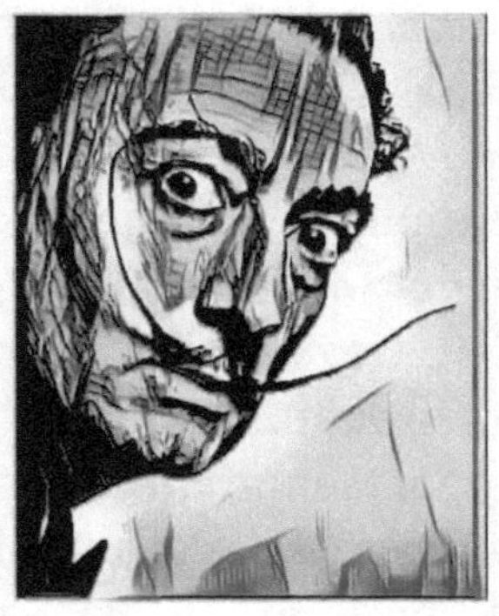

Key to Salvador Dali's art is his pursuit of concretization of dreams. This involves a credible breach in the civilizational habit of taking reality as a fixed entity. Art such as this has to be hyper real in details. This exactness of minute attributes is fraught with danger as modern art abhors photo-realism and definitely the spatial illusion is a raging anathema in the canon of modern art. This is a testimony to 'freakish talent' of Dali that he pulled off the audacious artistic coup of 'renaissance like modern art'.

His New York Times obituary in January 1989, while talking of Dali's virtuosity and his abilities as a 'high-concept painter', said "by his involvement with that modernist taboo, spatial illusionism. Dali did not simply resurrect Renaissance perspective. He used it as it had never quite been used before, to delineate an immense emptiness that was both terrifying and seductive, infinite and exact." "There was nothing he could not do in the way of exactitude: When the occasion called for a representation of a landscape, a seascape, a skyscape, a beautiful woman, a loaf of bread or an expensive watch, he did it to perfection in a style that was all reassurance. Only after a closer look did it become clear that the watch had gone soft like overripe Camembert, that very peculiar things were happening to the beautiful woman, and that it would be a mistake to put too much trust in the lyrical perfection of the land and the sea and the sky. Realism for the Unreal World" said another mourner when he passed away.

"We Surrealists are not artists," he is quoted to have said "Nor are we really scientists. We are caviar, and caviar is the extravagance and the very intelligence of taste." This "very intelligence of taste" was a result of his talent that collided with the rampaging intellectual landscape of his time. He was evolving and prospering in one of the most stimulating times. Communism, fascistic thought schools, capitalism in political economic areas, world wars, scientific developments and new ideas in social sciences and humanities impacted him very deeply.

Of the quartet of Modern Masters of 20th Century i.e. Picasso, Matisse, Dali and Warhol, only Dali has shown influence of reigning ideas or even ideologies in some discernible fashion. Picasso, though a member of Communist Party, was remarkably untouched by the events of his day. His Guernica is one of the few paintings that inspire comment on the happenings of the day. Matisse, the painter of refuge and luxury lived in one of the most difficult times during French occupation but his paintings do not carry even the slightest trace of commentary on the events of the time. Warhol benefitted from the contemporary feel of his work by painting the icons of his time but he is not about representation but about presentation. He is not propagating anything, just putting a frame to things and elevating them to the level of art. Dali, on the other hand, is an illustrator of the ideas that shaped the first 75 years of the last century. His paintings are a virtual encyclopedia of the ideas like Psycho-analysis started by the great Sigmund Freud. He found many explanations of his sexual and existential anxieties in the concepts of psychoanalysis. He found strong justification for his fascination with sexual inadequacy, threat from father figures and almost morbid allure of death. Things which were the cause of his pathological shyness in his adolescence became a badge of honour for him in his later years. Similarly, scientific leaps in quantum physics also found literal representation in his output. Here his fascination rested on the possibility of an alternate reality, a deeper more nuanced reality which could be imagined by a contradictory combination of ultra-realistic attention to details and taking a flight of imagination that is totally oblivious of rules of Newtonian rationality. With all his bizarre other worldliness he remains a child of his times. These developments encouraged dreamlike output while grappling with the expression of 'true reality'. Advent of cinema also accentuated this rising respect for non-rational, dream-like representation of reality. At that time they may not look very realistic but definitely alerted fertile minds to experiment away from the reigning notion of modernity.

Dali collaborated with Luis Buñuel on two of the underground classics of 20th century film, Un Chien Andalou (An Andalusian Dog) and L'Age d'Or (The Golden Age); he was more in sync with the dynamics of cinematic reality than any other painter of his day, "partly because he was obsessed by the power of cinema to make dreams immediate" Hitchcock also used him for his dream sequence in Spellbound. He was, like Picasso, taking away the layers of veneers that were obfuscating the reality by venturing into absolutely new ways of depicting it. Difference was what he was doing with the tools given to him by the intellectual climate of his times.

Whenever he realized the promise of this complex baggage, the results have been truly great. His 'dreamlike quality' of cinema was obtained in The Persistence of Memory, 1929, with the softness of watches, seemingly unrelated stench of death and an atmosphere of serene morbidity has made it one of the most famous paintings of all time. Paranoiac-Astral Image, 1934 illustrates his psyco-analytical obsession in all its majesty. On a vast and empty wilderness of a beach four images are dispersed. "A fragment of an amphora suggests "deep" time, the Greco-Roman past of the Catalan coast. A distant woman, perhaps the constantly remembered nurse of Dali's childhood, is almost bleached out by the sunlight. In a stranded boat, another woman, probably his muse and wife Gala, confronts a boy in a sailor suit who can be none other than Dali himself. And on the left, the hated figure of Dali's father strides along in a three-piece suit, casting a long shadow" says Robert Hughes. You are literally reading a book by Sigmund Freud. 'Dali's greatest and most frightening work: the Soft Construction with Boiled Beans--Premonition of Civil War, 1936." Is counted among the most eloquent anti-war artwork of all times, even, according to many, surpasses Picasso's Guernica. Let me quote Hughes again "with this single painting, Dali moved into the territory of Goya. This monstrous Titan in the act of tearing itself to pieces is the most powerful image of a country's anguish and dismemberment to issue from Spain (or anywhere else) since Goya's Desastres and Disparates. And every inch of it, from the sinister greenish clouds and electric-blue sky to the gnarled bone and putrescent flesh of the monster, is exquisitely painted. This, not Picasso's Guernica, is modern art's strongest testimony on the Spanish Civil War." Remember Robert Hughes is no fan of Dali. After all, it is all about the intelligence of taste.

A review of Matisse's 'The Dance' vis-a-vis Picasso's 'Les Demoiselles d'Avignon'

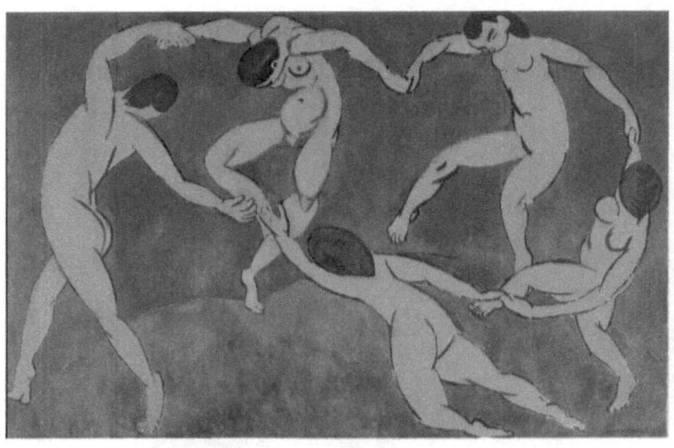

Matisse has traversed the extremes of primal depths to posh sophistication of civilization with his supernatural mastery over colours. While he excelled in uber urban 'window' paintings or in the crimson modernism of the 'Red Studio', he touched the very dawn of civilization in its entire primitive glory in, arguably, the greatest Matisse 'The Dance'. In both the cases his sophistication as well barbaric impulses have one source– colour. With him, colours are the raw material of feelings, a base material to be splashed to create a wide ranging continuum of moods and sensibilities. Whether it is the assault of red or ethereal hues of 'The Dance,' he is playing with chromatic nuances to convey his mood and underlying sensitivities that make him such a huge master. I will stick to 'The Dance' here as this painting has its place right in the crucible of the modern art revolution that started with the jolt of 'Les Demoiselles d'Avignon' by Picasso in 1906-07. Art was never the same for anyone, but for Matisse, 'the Fauve-wild beast' the shock was more stinging and he was looking for a suitable riposte to reach his natural perch i.e. at the very frontier of the art revolution.

Ace critic Robert Hughes has termed The Dance as "one of the few wholly convincing images of physical ecstasy made in the twentieth century." This is undoubtedly true for almost any other epoch of art. Hermitage Museum explains on its website that the painting acquired its 'famous passion and expressive resonance' in its final version, a reference to subdued MoMA version i.e. Dance-I where pink bodies do not unleash 'volcano of energy'. 'The frenzy of the pagan bacchanalia is embodied in the powerful, stunning accord of red, blue and green, uniting Man, Heaven and Earth' continues Hermitage website.

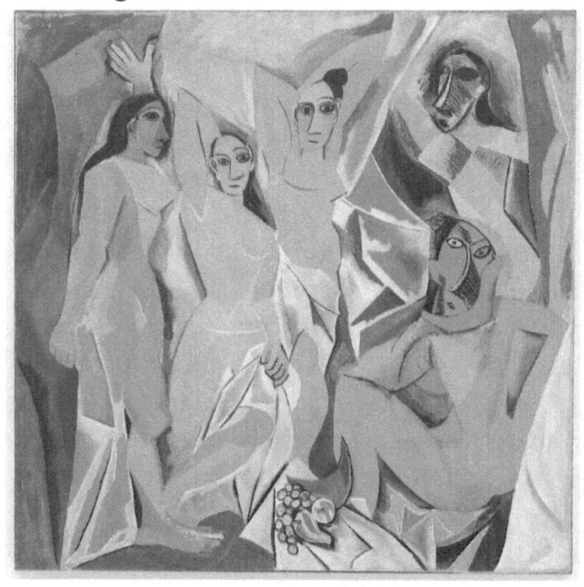

With its cave-painting purity The Dance scores over the African origins of 'Les Demoiselles d'Avignon'. Break from tradition that was a whiplash in the Picasso masterpiece became a deep-rooted, ever present reality with the self-contained burst of energy with Matisse painting. In one of the most exciting decades of modern art, rules were being rewritten. Fauves under Matisse had already moved away from the outside reality. They were painting what was seen by them or how it was imprinted in their fertile imaginations. Their skin tones could be of any hue, their beaches could be yellow or anything could be anything that is why they were the 'wild beasts'. Picasso brought a new reality, a reality that was a radical reconstruction of the form. He really took the game to a different level and opened a completely new vista for experimenters. Here ferocity and distortion were the key novelties that were challenging the time honoured traditions of painting. A newly globalised world had opened African aesthetics to Europe. Picasso, the creative predator, made the most radical use of it. Shock of 'Les Demoiselles d'Avignon' took some time to register. Even Picasso did not display the painting for some time. Matisse along with his Russian patron Sergei Shchukin was among the viewers who understood the game-changing value of the masterpiece. Matisse clearly saw a rival and Picasso was to enter in the same mood three years later when Matisse came back with a far more radical but understated mutation of the aesthetic tradition.

"Both paintings present the same number of nudes, but where Picasso painted five women who challenge you the viewer, Matisse answers him with a picture whose five naked inhabitants don't care if you are there or not" says Jonathan Jones of the Guardian. Picasso is aggressive, Matisse self-contained. Picasso is brazenly engaging you with a defiant stare. He is abrasive and violence is directed not only on the nude female bodies but on the viewer too in the equal amount. Here he is firmly ensconced in the tradition of European art, a tradition of painting pulling in the viewer with direct stare. Here the full impact of art is dependent on the reaction of the viewer. Mona Lisa does it. Even where the stare is not directed on the viewer, a clear cut stage like feeling is there, demanding reverence, lust, disgust or submission for completing the aesthetic experience. Picasso breaks many canons of the artistic tradition with his ferocity and distortion but he is dependent on the viewer. He is trying to establish a dialogue with her, though from an offensive, brazen and violent perch. The Dance, on the other hand, is self-contained. It is a scene that stands on its own, its own energy, its own joy, its own ecstasy. This is a private revelry whose link with the viewer is tenuous. The experience of watching this masterpiece is at once submerging and distant. It washes over you with perfect harmony of colours and it distances itself with its indifference. Its remoteness is its reaffirmation of its revolutionary provenances. Jonathan Jones puts it very aptly "Dance is modernist in a way that has not faded. When you look at it, you are unsettled as well as uplifted. It seems on the edge of emptiness."

This 'edge of emptiness' is full of pure colours to use Jones again "there's nothing in any other painting quite like the chromatic miracle of Dance. Terracotta flesh combines mysteriously in your mind with those saturated blues and greens, in a poem of absolutes. Absolute red, absolute blue, absolute green - a hymn of intensity." Matisse knew that his riposte to 'Les Demoiselles d'Avignon' had to be through colours as the savage formal revolution of the Picasso masterpiece was beyond any riposte. It was a new realm of form distorted through the eye of the Spanish genius. It stood on its own and any competition to it would have been a meek duplication or insipid follow up. Matisse drew a different line. It was pure energy unleashed by the purity of tones. Very limited but intense tones. The Master himself is known to say ""the surface was coloured to saturation, to the point where blue, the idea of absolute blue, was conclusively present. A bright green for the earth and a vibrant vermilion for the bodies. With these three colours I had my harmony of light and also purity of tone." The alchemy was complete.

La Danse or The Dance was commissioned by Sergei Shchukin for the grand staircase of his palatial residence in Moscow. It was a two painting commission i.e. for La Danse (Dance) and La Musique (Music) in 1909. The Russian was hesitant about the nude dancers but after seeing the water sketch he came round. On completion, these paintings were savaged by the critics and people even doubted Matisse's sanity. A shaken Shchukin visited Paris and surrendered to the vociferous criticism and cancelled the commission. On his two-day journey back to Moscow, he reconsidered his position. The enlightened tycoon wrote to Matisse ""I've thought things over and I'm ashamed of my weakness and lack of courage. ..... I have decided to hang your panels. People may shout and laugh, but since I'm convinced that your path is the right one, perhaps time will be my ally and I shall claim victory in the end". He was the proud owner of the two masterpieces till the revolution in 1917. Westerners could see the paintings only in 1969. Shchukin had the last laugh.

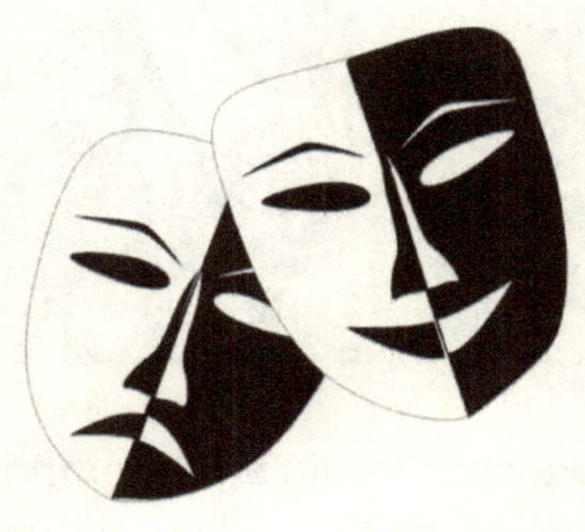

Moulded by Kisses and Caresses: Warm Flesh of Rodin's Sculpture

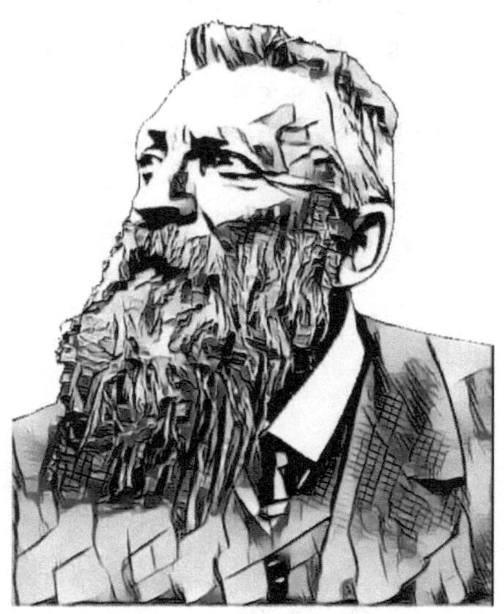

When Augustus Rodin's contemporaries in painting were transcending naturalism to ring in modernity in painting, he was literally chiselling away habits of classicism to push sculpture to modernity. Sculpture, by definition, has a brute materiality about it. This materiality helped prolong the grand themes of classicism – stability, mythical subjects and a condensed other worldliness

– longer than, say, painting or music. It fell on Rodin to bring in movement, fleeting moments, unfinished surfaces, in other words – 'embrace of ambiguity' through ' a conflicted allegiance to grandiosity and intimacy.'

Rodin has been labelled as grandiose, ostentatious and even corny. His reputation dipped immediately after his death in 1917 when the new breed of sculptor (many of whom worked under him eg.. Maillol, Brancusi, Bourdelle, Pompon etc.) started preferring 'meaningful Canons of form & Vision' over Rodin's searing emotions expressed by hyper detailing. While benefiting from Rodin's paving of the way from classical themes, they focused their own voices on achieving a less detailed or complicated form, reaching core in a quieter way. Today, however, Rodin stands as an undisputed harbinger of modernity in sculpture, often compared to Michelangelo in impact and stature.

Classicism was grand and sure. A realized truth with scriptural certainty. It conveyed a fully formed reality cast in stone. This was called 'monumentality' i.e. representation of completeness of a divinity, an era, impact of king, nobleman or a mistress. Rodin who had ready access to the art of the past. Found a potent weapon to subvert the grand tradition. This weapon was doubt. He was lucky to be at the intersection of '19th century amplitude' & '20th century doubt'. His equivocation, his insistence on capturing the fleeting moment — a work in progress sensibility brought a rupture. A rupture that is brought forth only by an epoch — shaping artists.

His 'anti-monumentalism' was a natural corollary of his stubborn rejection of completeness. In 'Les Bourgeois de Calais', a depiction of six wealthy citizens of the French town who offered themselves to the attacking army for execution as a price for safety of their fellow citizens, the moment that Rodin chose to depict was neither the surrender nor the execution (which never took place) but a moment when they were alone after the spark of initial heroism had passed. The art work is not recreating a landmark moment but a void with a promise of movement and uncertainty. Doom, despair and surrender to fate is still a work in progress before getting to its horrible, chaotic finality.

This rejection of completeness reached a new level during his mature years in works like hands or headless torsos. These disembodied works left scope for possibilities. The telos, the final cause remained hidden but, quite clearly, the moving force in this melee of incompleteness. A moving force propelled by entropy and renewal. Robert Hughes found in these incomplete figures 'expressive power of the non-finito' and savage force of the human form to express emotion. Hughes wrote "his use of the "partial figure"—the headless striding man, the ecstatically capering figure of Iris, Messenger of the Gods—went beyond such conventions as the body not yet released from its mass of raw stone, or even the broken antique fragment. It was a way of asserting the power of reduction, a demonstration that the expressive power of human form could be so concentrated as to drop, without loss, such usual signifiers of emotion as the head." Incompleteness is a sure indicator of movement. This kinetic fuel is another hallmark of the break that Rodin effected from stable unmoving glory of classicism. Unfinished conundrum of Iris, Messenger of the Gods or Walking Man and his distinctive musculature created tension in his stones or bronze that signified movement. Talking about this kinetic appeal in the 'Walking Man' Peter Schjendahl of The New Yorker wrote "Walking becomes lurching. The effect is simple, but it electrifies as the sign of an intelligence that comprehends, and can gainfully subvert, the fictive language of figuration in sculpture. You get, in a flash, that Rodin could have played no end of Picasso-like games with givens of the medium, had he been more of a sophisticate."

While his transmogrifying and cross feeding sculpture reminded of Picasso's inventiveness, his most potent playfield was flesh - the surface. Rodin said "to any artist worthy of the name, all in nature is beautiful, because his eyes, fearlessly accepting all extension truth, read there, as is an open book, all the inner truth". There he is closest to the great British artist Lucian Freud, for whom flesh was 'mound of feelings'. This fascination with speaking flesh has brought forth a sexual frankness in both Freud's and

Rodin's work. While Freud kept on working the texture and tone of his model's flesh, Rodin's surfaces are his most thoroughly finished incompleteness. Gaping sexuality of 'Iris the Messenger of God' fascinates more by pulsating coarseness of the texture then its exposed boldness. He achieved a very real surface for his work. His ideal was captured by Paul Gsell. Rodin when talking of Venus de Medici, swooned "It is truly flesh! You would think it was moulded by kisses and caresses! You almost expect, when you touch this body, to find it warm". This 'warm' flesh is one more definitive indicator of his subversion of Classicism, a period of idealized surfaces. His reputation for eroticism often bordered on sensationalism. His quest to recover 'freedom of instinct' led to many experimentations which were even termed 'exploitative' use of his models. For Rodin there was no visual compromise, he sought to avoid stage effect in his nudes. 'I know why my drawings have this intensity. It is because I do not intervene. Between nature and paper, I eliminated talent. I do not reason. I simply let myself go." Like Goya, like Picasso and like Matisse, Rodin exemplifies the primal force of nature where talent appears eliminated simply by its pervasiveness. Rodin is an undisputed master and his absence for the last hundred years has made it clear beyond any doubt.

Breaking Bad: First Among Equals

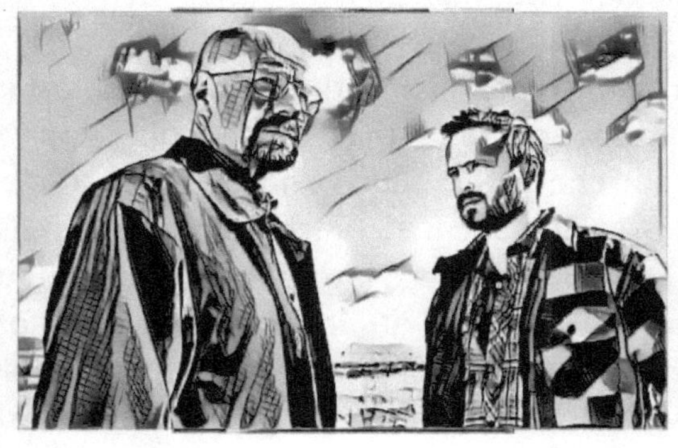

After all these years, much of the technical superiority of Breaking Bad does not look so unassailable. Breath taking photography, emotion-appropriate editing, use of topography- making the landscape a protagonist, using heartbreakingly normal situations to enact epic questions of humanity and great acting have become rather common and do not count for insurmountable strategic advantage. Great TV in Fargo, The Fall, Luther, True Detective, Orange is the New Black etc have amply demonstrated that these aspects, though making for a sustained advantage, are replicable with similar success. Then, what makes a series like Breaking Bad a classic, first among equals and account for such a high degree of sustained cult popularity coupled with mainstream acclaim?

Answer to my mind is that none of the other contenders have this dense collection of great characters. Each and every character of Breaking Bad is significant enough to have a personality and interesting background story worthy of an independent spin off series- Better Call Saul is one highly rewarding example. Though Walt and Jesse get most of the screen time and their character ticks are most microscopically presented, none of the significant characters are peripheral. Mike, Gustav Frig, Skyler, Hank, Marie, Todd, Lydia or the kids (including the infant-Holly), and, of course, Saul Goodman have been invested with strong personalities. They are all people who make for great partners but never can be relegated to the status of a tool or paid employee. Bit characters like Uncle Jack of Todd or the Vacuum guy, Badger and Skinny Pate have a quality of permanence that carries them through for a very long series spanning over five seasons. Other series too have memorable characters and some of them are permanent fixtures of   TV pantheon but Vince Gilligan has created an unprecedented constellation of great characters and placed them in a perfect story. Command over the progression of the story- often tricky in long series, is pitch perfect and creates a narrative which forces the viewers to stay invested in the fates of the characters.

A character grows on the audience in the alchemy of paradox. The character needs to be immediately clear also and it should have an element of surprise — joy of deciphering or unraveling. Gustav Frig is a character that has coiled neatness about him. We know he has more to him than meets the eye. We take delight in discovering his backstory, innate decency, capacity for violence or capacity for revenge. Mike too portrays his reliable solidity immediately but we take pleasure in discovering his languid approach, his softer aspects, his supreme efficiency in what he does. Hank comes as an amiable lout of a detective. His detective skills and absolute incorruptibility is immediately evident. We love his tenacity and fragility. Ladies, Skyler, Marie and Lydia have fully developed character arcs complete with flaws and undiluted capacity to give. Lydia's greed, absolute self-centeredness and paranoid ambition simply shine through in the limited number of scenes that she had. Todd's type gets established in efficient strokes and a high functioning sociopath was established in a few quick scenes. In short, strong characterization is the main strength of this much awarded show and a quality that can't be copied very easily.

Other technical virtues, mentioned in the beginning may be easy to copy but their standard in Breaking Bad is nothing short of outstanding. Spare, sparse landscape of New Mexico complements the rugged mood of the topic and creates a neo western aura around the show which serves it well. Photography and editing are elegant and their cleverness contributes and doesn't distract. Angle shots from inside the safe, barrels, table top etc add urgency. Close ups, play with depths, wipes are plenty but never come in the way of storytelling and only add to the atmosphere.

The mixture of operatic ambition in technical aspects, epic aspirations in latent messages on the one hand and resolute everydayness of the settings worked well for the show. The family, household, neighborhood, office, car wash, dresses, bit characters at gas stations, department stores and look and feel was kept real. Sense of grandeur came from the sweep of story, photography and far reaching changes that the situations brought in the characters. This has a quality of great literature- almost Shakespearean.

Even for a binge watch, the show did not lose its story thread and one cannot but marvel at the impeccable continuity and controlled arch of the story. Breaking Bad is compelling television, the best of its kind. It will continue to attract lovers of quality TV for a long time.

Fleabag: Heartbreakingly funny

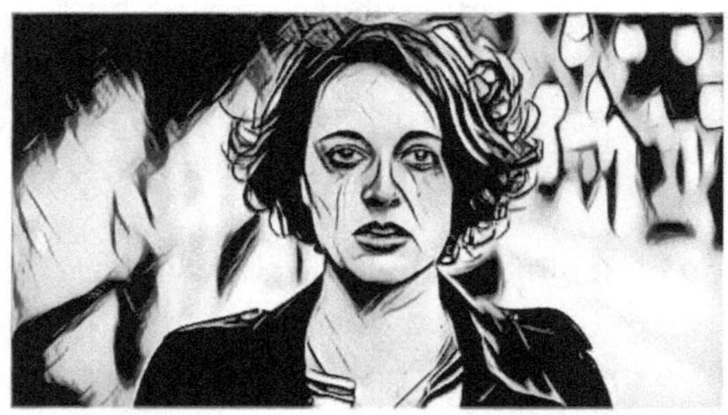

Fleabag, a two season BBC drama, achieves greatness by subordinating its all too ostentatious brilliance to the core task of story-telling. It is no mean feat, when the show is overflowing with talented actors, scene-stealers all. List of individually dazzling elements is long, snappy lines, great acting, great use of turning to the audience - opening of the fourth wall (deployed with great felicity by Kevin Spacey in House of Cards) and tight editing (all episodes are below 30 min in 6 episode a season series). All these can easily turn into self-serving clever ploys attracting attention to their elegance and distracting from the inherent story line. Instead, what happens is that those maddening tempo scenes, those fourth wall tricks, those relentlessly funny repartee, compulsive humour trip, overwrought mania, imposition of intimate and flashbacks are all breathing and stopping to create the whiplash of the intended impact marked for that point in the story of grieving girl who is trying to make sense of her needs, her guilt and her desires while making a life in London and trying to relate to her family in a uniquely complicated way. Her success and failure is beside the point but it is one hilarious journey of glorious chaos, heartbreaks and shocking poignancy. In the second season the father, at a particularly taxing dinner, asks the Fleabag (many characters have not been given names and Amazon subtitles has done a marvellous job of giving nicknames like Hot Priest, Arsehole guy, Hot Misogynist etc) "not being naughty", the banter between the father and the daughter goes breezily and she says "it doesn't matter". In that simple moment we understand the growth, costs and damage that has taken place. The girl who was marked as difficult presence and managed to ruin many a situation without intending to be such a wrecking force, finds herself not giving a damn. The aforementioned elements were serving the story.

Bad girl stories with shocking vocabulary is dime a dozen but very few rise above mush and pretentious display of some ideological points. Fleabag retains understated intelligence despite being over the top in deploying its arsenal. Fleabag, the heroine is vivacious and intelligent but she never goes for cheap cutesy points. Her issues, her exposition of those issues and her understanding is so deep and so lived in that they are saved from the horrific destiny of eyelash flattering cute crap. She remains gorgeous and real. In one of the many sex scenes where she keeps on talking to us, she tellingly says "stay sexy, always stay sexy". And we understand that she is in sync with the banality of it all. She is worried that she is not a good feminist but that too is used to convey her fierce independence. When she tells the character of Kirstin Scott Thomas that people are shit, Thomas' character depicted as a successful woman businessperson awardee that understands the infantile ghettoizing nature of such awards but still comes to take that, tells her "people are all we have got." At many levels, the wisdom of the show is a joy in itself.

When the first scene of the series involves a "spot of sodomy", it is easy to fall prey to the easy allure of titillating debauchery, especially when it comes from the gorgeously profane mouth of an attractive girl. The show maintains its relationship with the profane throughout but never allows it to stink and overpower the lilting momentum of the consummate story telling. Sex 'says' not 'sells' here.

There are some good series or movies involving intelligent men also. Sometimes deliciously debauch and sometimes just debauch. Californication comes to mind. Many Woody Allen starrer are good examples. Though in later appearances Woody Allen suffered from the tendency of being rather too aware of his cleverness. Happens with the best of them. Self-caricature is a difficult boogie to shake off. Fleabag is spot on for being clever without taking it too seriously.

The series is a high point among TV offerings. The description of the show on Amazon is to the point "a dry-witted woman, known only as Fleabag, has no filter as she navigates life and love in London while trying to cope with tragedy. The angry, grief-riddled woman tries to heal while rejecting anyone who tries to help her, but Fleabag continues to keep up her bravado through it all. Comic actress Phoebe Waller-Bridge stars as the titular character on the series, which is based on Waller-Bridge's 2013 one-woman show of the same name." Centrality of Phoebe is well earned and she delivers a stunning performance-layered and brave. However, great performances are commonplace in this superlative show. Apart from the main protagonist, there is a great ensemble cast of solid names of British TV and stage. Andrew Scott (Moriarty in Cumberbatch's Sherlock.), Olivia Colman, Bill Paterson, Sian Clifford are all superb as expected.

At another level, the show is a matter of great satisfaction. We are beginning to sense the deterioration caused by algorithm driven offerings of the streaming services. It is becoming difficult to commit to a series as tropes are too clear, inherent grammar too obvious to veteran viewers. BBC gave three great miniseries around the same time, taut

Bodyguard and Collateral and Fleabag. In the last few years the best 'cinematic' work has happened on television. The format of TV series has attracted the best of the minds (Fargo, 24, Sopranos, Breaking Bad, Mad Man, True Detective the list is endless)and much of the budget also. It is important that we keep on seeing such satisfying fructification of the effort as this great series.

That sexy beast Jude Law is playing Pope- The Young Pope

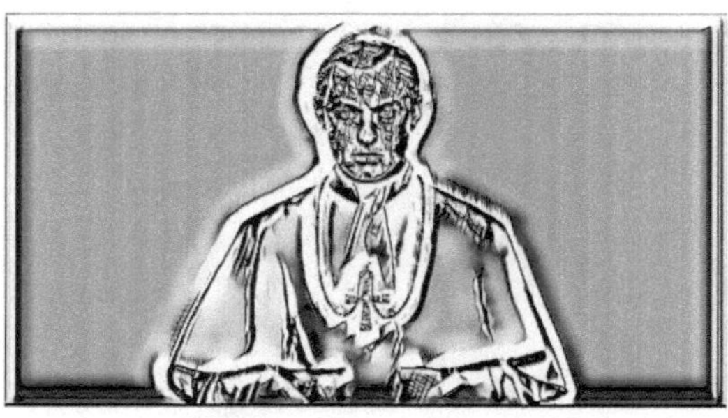

Europe does it for me. Italy or to be more precise, Rome surely does it for me. Anything set in the locale simply ignites the mood for quirky bohemia. Any level of sophistication stops being snobbish. Art and highbrow conversation seem normal. Then there is the Vatican. A mythical city-state erected on a tomb. A symbol that can really be leveraged to heighten any emotion, be it conspiracy, power play or simply eye-watering spiritualism laced miracle mongering. Expectant, devoted, enchanted faces are simply part of the scenery. Awe is an easy state to reach in such situations. Woody Allen and Dan Brown (films on his books) have used both the bohemian and the awe elements with great felicity. But I digress.

That sexy beast Jude Law is playing Pope- a Young Pope. He is a nightmare for people trying to get out of their smoking habits. Surely, he uses the fag with great oomph. His loose charms, coiled but accessible, are ready to enliven any conceit that Oscar winning Director Paolo Sorrentino conjures to tell a story of an intriguing but vacant idea. But I digress.

Jude is not the only charisma melting the screen. There is Diane Keaton. She is so posh that even in habit she is unbearably stylish. Her nightshirt is a riot (I am a virgin...but that's an old story), shoes with appealing heels and the walk of a sophisticated CEO. Verve, solidity and great acting make her a treat to watch. She is a star. But I digress

Silvio Orlando as Cardinal Angelo Voiello, Camerlengo and Cardinal Secretary of State is the fulcrum of the show. In some episodes you get a feeling that he is getting more screen time than Jude Law. He is one stout bundle of contradictions. He brings easy comedy, always a tall order, and chutzpah to his role as solid servant of the church. However, his service aspects are deeply hidden as he is a scheming politician and admits to it. A solid and believable performance that is often infused with audacious naughtiness. Again, I digress. There is so much in the show that can make one digress from the beauty of the full package.

The Young Pope is simply great because it is lyrical filmmaking so typical of great Italian directors from Michelangelo Antonioni, Federico Fellini and others. Great performances are a given. Here, Paolo Sorrentino is in good form. His films are funny and maintain a rhythm that traces not only the mood arch of the key protagonist in this case, Jude Law's Pope, but also has capacity to go whimsy, surreal or plain fun at will. His greatest strength is to take a given moment and create something really enjoyable. Examples aplenty. Pope getting ready to vaguely blasphemous background music (I am sexy, I know it), Secretary of state contemplating Venus of Willendorf, again the Secretary of State following a football match dressed in the team uniform, Pope's dealings with uptight Vatican bureaucracy. Every episode is full of memorable moments Sister Antonia in Africa was painted in very deft free strokes, Pope's media officer, his two confidantes are all not only viable but enjoyable too. Portrayal of innate mysterious powers of the Pope despite his obviously mundane power games are so fine tuned that sympathy remains with him despite his militant anachronistic views.

Storyline is mostly known by now. A 46 year old American Cardinal Lenny Belardo, has been elected as Pope and established powers are imagining a pliable puppet. Rest of the story is how this situation is tackled by the new Pope. He takes an unorthodox approach to ensure his supremacy while advocating fundamentalist orthodoxy of the Catholic Church. Another omnipresent overhang is his mommy issue. As a child he was abandoned by his Hippie parents. The Pope is obsessed with this issue. His detractors say that it is affecting his decision-making.

A word about Jude Law. The actor in the tradition of Downey Jr (Sherlock to his Watson) and Johnny Depp, is a good tool of engaging flippancy and irreverence. His good looks don't distract but enhance the contradictions of his situation in the show. He is in sure directorial hands and his timing is impeccable. He is amused, horrified, intrigued and evil with consummate ease. His whining for mommy is surprisingly not very irritating. His heartbreak, solitude and sorrow are sublime. When he cries after the death of his spiritual father and chief competitor (a superb James Cromwell), it is primal and tears our heart out. His star aura is a chief prop for a show that is so openly wedded to extrovert pointing to its own cleverness.

The show is full of itself, in a good sort of way, exuberance and overt highbrow approach is sustained with unfailing direction quality and impeccable production values. Whenever opulence becomes obscenely lavish, it serves a story purpose. It has been said that the show likes its own voice too much, but then, there is a lot to like there. We do enjoy the beats of electro music that is deployed to perk up a moment.

No doubt that the premise, while being interesting and intriguing, is flimsy and it is difficult to sustain for 10 lengthy episodes. You can face only that many court intrigues, that many clever strategies to impose your will or keep impressing with arcane, splendid and mythical beauties of the world's most famous religious seat. This is great material for a feature length movie (Dan Brown films are examples) but a series is a difficult proposition. Sorrentino has manfully handled this problem and his solution is to convey that the characters in the show, despite their exaggerated uniqueness, are not one-dimensional characters. He takes his time to show the hidden aspects of these characters.

Jude Law, while conveying impetuous distracted charm, starts showing real saintly characteristics. The Secretary of State, while being an opportunistic and scheming politician comes out with a much deeper multilayered personality that is deeply devoted to his church. The same is true for other notables. Investigation of the child abuse scandal brought thriller element and sustained the momentum of the show at a critical juncture. The length of the show provides an appropriate platform to fathom the depth and peeling off layers of these characters. In the hands of a director like Sorrentino, this becomes a joyful journey as he infuses it with panache and unpredictable twists. The show never loses its funny core. A memorable outing to the small screen by a proven master of celluloid.

Review of True Detective Season 1: Engaging Dark Core of an Intelligent Show

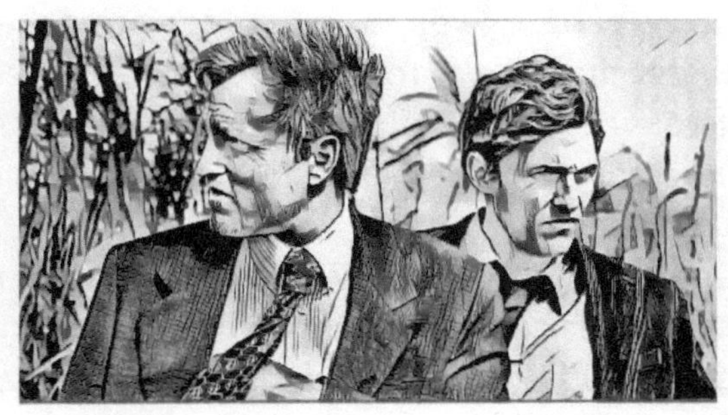

'True Detective' tells a complicated grisly crime story with details, very good acting and atmospherics. It seems that this-straight forward story telling of a spectacular crime, is reason enough to catapult the star-studded HBO show to stratospheric heights of popularity. But that is not the only reason for this to be an outstanding show. It has a strong subject matter depicted with gritty control over the narrative. Presence of the 'two masters of laconic' Woody Harrelson and Matthew McConaughey has knitted the story in the overall aura of excellence.

Top notch performances by McConaughey and Harrelson are the key pleasure of this very enjoyable show. McConaughey, who is in the sweet spot of creative and professional resurgence has hogged the limelight. In fact, singular in the title is for him. He has given a great performance-taught and good to watch. He remained clued into the ruined grandeur of his character. In both young and later parts he managed to convey the anguish of a damaged soul which is aware enough to grasp the horror of its own decay. This doomed intelligence and doggedness that was sure and righteous, got beautifully showcased in the star persona of a great actor. But my vote goes to that magnificent creep, Woody Harrelson. He was not transferring a one-dimensional trauma but a whole array of sensibilities. He was flawed in a much more nuanced way. His Marty is far more layered in conveying the real fault lines of an inherently decent man prone to envy and adultery. He had to convey decency while playing second fiddle, not a particularly difficult task. Dr Watson in his many avatars has done it manfully over the years. But here Marty has to create a story by being a force rather than a prop. The bromance or buddy angle apart, he is not in awe of McConaughey's Cohle. He does not have the ultimate clutch of loyalty card. He is there as a player not as a sidekick. He, unlike Cohle, is not functioning with a given tune of tormented philosopher. He is being equally impactful in a more mundane mantle. In the absence of showy props (tragic backstory, ruined look, past as soul-shattering undercover agent) his spectacular performance gets more weight.

Despite dealing with universal themes, 'True Detective' has a provincial core. It is not easily accessible to a non-American. Louisiana landscape and accented monologue will need a second viewing for a person like me to get the full flavor. However, the genius of the show is clear. This is a highly moody and individualistic take on a conventional hunt of a murderer by two detectives who, despite their damaged selves, retain a true passion to fight the darkness of crime. The plot is simple. 'True Detective' follows the Louisiana State Police detectives Rust Cohle (Matthew McConaughey) and Marty Hart (Woody Harrelson) as they investigate a series of occult-based sex murders in the course of seventeen years. Smattering of occult references and nuanced deflecting of suspicion have kept cyberspace abuzz with the discussion about the series. A good cultural product is supposed to create discussion and disagreement. Here we have plenty.

There are sequences which stand out. Six minute long take in an action sequence at the end of episode four has been rated 'worthy of Scorsese.' Final episode had the climax that was very creepy and gave a fitting finale to the sickness that pervaded throughout the series. Family scenes, interrogations, bonding sequences, chases etc fitted in the whole that the creator planned for them.

However, I liked many other shows better, particularly from the UK and Scandinavia. Maybe 'True Detective' is getting more attention due to the pop philosophical air that it managed to gather, big banner and heavyweight starcast. The show is smart enough to avoid spoofs that such ultra serious pieces evoke so easily. Maybe not smart enough, as The New Yorker has taken upon itself to find what is funny and 'hot air' in the show. Truth be told, I am slightly wary of the critics who start with a gender angle, which might be very important in itself but of limited value as a device for an objective review. On a different level, deep understanding may often deprive you of simple pleasures. It may lead to compulsive spoofing without appreciation of the good elements. That said, 'True Detective' is superlative TV and pushes the envelope in many departments of the genre. Clichés will be there, that is why we go back to a genre. 'True Detective' does a splendid job of presenting those clichés in an entertainingly intelligent way.

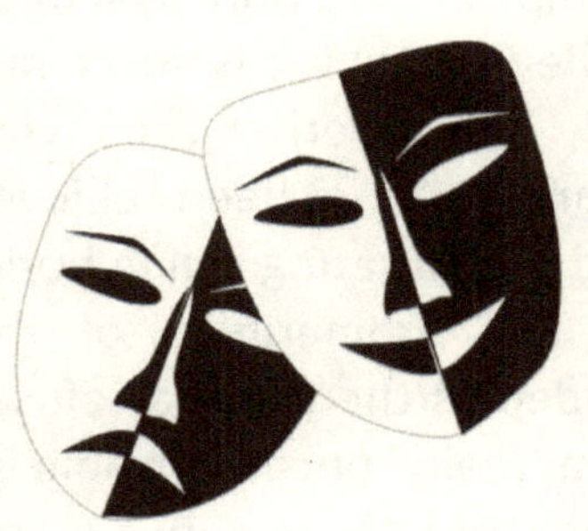

Normal Pathology of The Fall

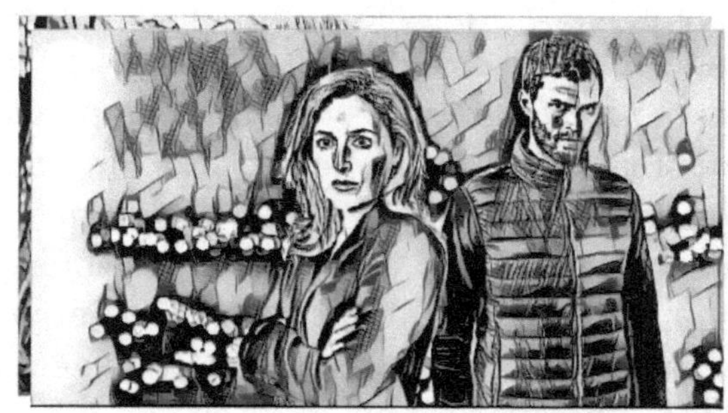

The Fall (BBC 2 starring Gillian Anderson and Jamie Dornon) is a great complex psychological drama. Allan Cubitt's drama is a serious affair with brilliant performances and uncompromising portrayal of evil. It is a difficult viewing which is scary rather than repelling. An overhang of violence or implicit threat has not been achieved by gore and blood but situating evil in boring sedate reality. This ordinariness of the evil is compounded as the camera refuses to turn away from 'really' uncomfortable issues.
"The basic story of the series is that of two hunters: a serial killer on the loose in Belfast and the police officer who is tasked with stopping him. The first hunter is a man by the

name of Paul Spector (Jamie Dornan); a serial killer who happens to be a grief counsellor by day. The second hunter is Detective Superintendent Stella Gibson (Gillian Anderson- she of X Files). Gibson, an officer from London's Metropolitan Police Service, is an old acquaintance of PSNI Assistant Chief Constable Jim Burns (John Lynch), who calls her in to do a 28 day review of a murder case which has stalled. While reviewing the case she comes across two cases which she believes are linked and were committed by the same individual and, after convincing Burns of that fact, abandons her review to head the inquiry into the serial killer on the loose in Belfast." (from TVwise review of the The Fall)

Serial killing is by definition sadistic i.e. killing for pleasure and, moreover, the victim has done nothing to earn her (mostly it is a she) fate except to conform to some characteristic that triggers the evil in the psychopath. In popular culture it has been used extensively however, almost always, a distance has been created by situating the evil in something exotic. Audiences differentiate themselves from serial killers in more fundamental ways than just degrees.

They normally don't see themselves on the same continuum and serial killers are given enough 'quirks' to make them a different species altogether. But not here. Proximity with the evil has been achieved not only with camera dwelling lovingly on the brutality but also the calm way in which the killer goes about his business at the crime scene.

More than this longish stay with the brutality, it is the context in which the killer has been put. Jamie Dornan's Paul Spector gets his menace quotient from the scenes in which he is placed in normal family life and a routine day job. Busy thrum and stress of the domesticity only adds to the normalcy of the circumstances. There is nothing extraordinary about the stress that he faces in his everyday life. He may not be cheerful but how many of normal people are? Still, there is no doubt that he is evil. Domesticity is a backdrop that props up his darker side. Use of deviant situations in routine everyday life creates an unease which does more to establish the dark canvas than the conventional mores of the suspense genre.

In one scene we meet Paul in his role as a grief counselor and find him asking probing questions to his clients. Occasional diversion in the sexual territory will not be noted, but from him it raises some antennas. Later we catch him making inappropriate drawings while the mother talks about the death of her child. Other uneasy situations involve children near perilous situations. He hides his gear in the false roof right above his son's bed, adorned with whatever children's rooms are adorned with. His daughter gives a jaunty family performance while he gets distracted by the news item about his previous kill. Inappropriate behavior of the teenage babysitter and her vulnerability in the presence of a cold blooded psychopath keeps us on edge. In a later scene, the camera follows the young daughter moving towards the room where Paul is wrestling with the babysitter.

These situations firmly established the perverse nature of the landscape. However, the perversity never crosses the line to become otherworldly. It always remains within the overall parameter of normalcy: just a point on the continuum where we all can see ourselves. Somehow, it always appears that this evil is possible for any one. Even the audience cannot rule itself out.

Another effective trick was a juxtaposition sequence in the beginning of the second episode. In the sequence camera alternately shifted between domineering lovemaking between DSI Stella and one of her subordinates and the languid perversion of the killer in which he 'poses' his victim with elaborate tenderness. The sequence serves to blur the boundaries of perverse behavior of a serial killer and seemingly normal behavior of DSI Stella. In short, intense atmospheric shots are used to stunning impact to give the series its calm eerie texture.

Performances are top notch. Gillian Anderson is effortless in conveying her haughtiness, maverick tendencies and a very strong personality. She uses the full weight of her personality to get what she wants — whether it is the attention of a good looking cop or to be lead investigator in a case. Above all she conveys her capabilities and vulnerability with great facility without making too much song and dance about them. The Fall achieves its status of being "perfect means of exploring the banality of evil, the nature of obsession, and the niggly-squirmy minutiae of everyday" by devoting equal time to the hunter and hunted. Jamie Dornon is playing the creepy with a surefootedness of a pro. He is able to survive long sequences without belaboring the point of his evil, still conveying the full horror of his 'normal' pathology.

Hannibal on TV- Cannibal in the living room

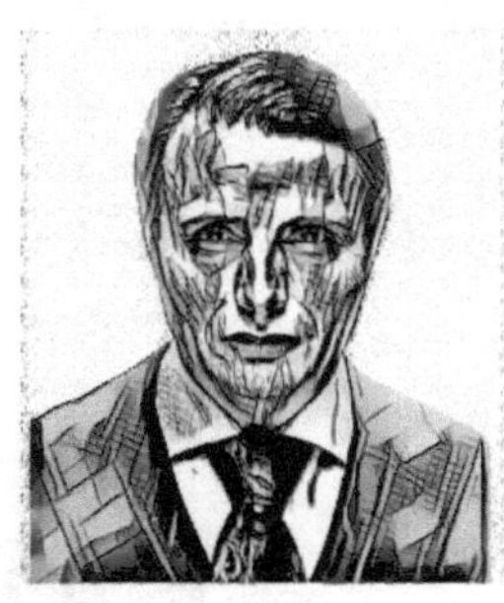

Dr. Hannibal Lecter is back on screen, this time on the small screen. As has been the wont of the genius cannibal doctor, he is the star of the show though, like always, most of the screen time is taken up by his pursuer the cop. In Hannibal, we are still at Red Dragon Lecter where he was still social, though ,actively engaged in his anti-social, anti-human activities of making homo-sapiens his lunch. In fact, Red Dragon and Silence of Lambs led to creation of an enduring villain who is a constant presence in background while centre stage is hogged by Will Graham in Red Dragon and Clarice Starling in the Silence. However, this dark fascination with evil followed the normal tendency of humanizing the evil and made him somewhat sympathize with dogged protagonists. Hannibal was made to care for Clarice a bit too much to retain the edge in his evil. Thomas Harris would have been better off just continuing to offer Lecter's genius and discomfort that he creates by his obvious superiority intertwined so effortlessly with his obvious evil.

 Great characters, whether suffering or inflicting sufferings, unravel when they start caring about other people. Brando's character in Last Tango in Paris was fascinating in his silent suffering and keeping the focus on his delicious agony. Bernardo Bertolucci in a masterly way showed how he lost his lustre once he became a normal 'sissy' boyfriend. You touch your dreams and they will change colour. Harris in effect killed the character with Hannibal (the third novel) and Hannibal Rising (The Last in series) effectively entombed the evil in the coffin of humanity.

This makes it interesting how the medium of TV, where the episode system provides new possibilities through the use of time that allows build up much more thoroughly than a two hour movie. On TV, Danish Actor Lars Mikkelsen took forward his poker strengths in Casino Royale. He is able to induce uncertainty in our feelings towards him. Uneasiness that his predilections create in our mind are easily compounded by his unwavering ambiguous gaze that conveys, more than anything, a disturbing quality of menace. The director is able to dexterously harness the food and eating connections of cannibalism. Scenes of unexplained sharing of food (with Will Graham in first episode and with Jack Crowford in second) with suspicious colour and texture add to this discomfort. Horror is more effective if it is repulsive in a more intimate way.

Apart from his culinary aspects, Hannibal is also indulging in 'breaking an interesting pony'. He relishes in mind games with a worthy opponent. Will Graham is a suitable challenge for his capabilities. In films and novels, Dr Lecter pulled his strings more subtly and explanations of his influence and reasoning were less obvious. On TV, this is done more elaborately. His rich understanding of human beings is on display and his effortless mental dual with Graham is part of the charm. Dr Lecter attains full traction only in the company of opponents who are unique in their own way. Will Graham and Clarice Starling both were special and damaged. Here, Will Graham's episodes of 'extreme empathy' are the dramatic high points which are used as a tool to unravel the gruesome montage that serial killers are so good at.   Hugh Dancy is burdened and suffering due to his gift. Dancy portrayed the vulnerability and determination with due felicity.

Build-up was promising as the show avoided haste in catching the audience. Similarly, character points for highlighting were identified and established with great success. Events and psychological duals carried the show.

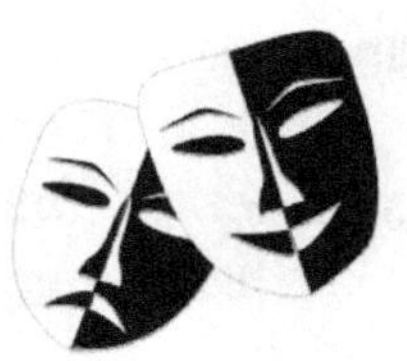

Rowan Atkinson: Understated Hyper Comedy

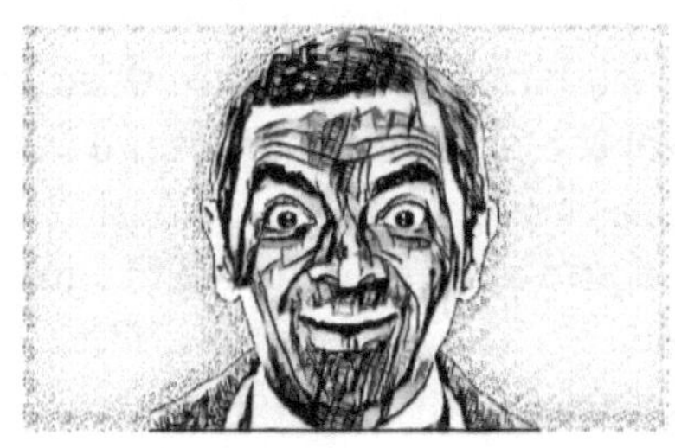

Rowan Atkinson is a rare commodity- a natural born actor. He is so pure a comedian that he personifies the character rather than enacting it. He chose comedy and stamped it with his subdued charisma. Ease and understatement are the chief ingredients of his genius. Understatement and Mr Bean. Sounds odd but Mr Bean or the character played by Atkinson is always in lower key. Any actor who has 'learnt' acting will play it in a much higher octave than an actor for whom acting is like breathing. With Atkinson this is a skill that is instinctive rather than honed.

This allows him to really compartmentalize. From available accounts, he is a very shy person with a passion for fast cars and a very private family life. He doesn't have to be a buffoon all the time as he can summon comedy at will. Tony Robinson, who played Baldrick in Blackadder with "cunning plan" fame told this to the Guardian, "he's one of the few mega performers who genuinely has a full and fulfilling life away from show business….. he remains for me the consummate comedy performer of his generation." Robinson added, "He's a very shy man, ….. When he's not working, you are unlikely to realise that he's in the room, but as soon as he starts, all attention focuses on him, partly because of this extraordinary supreme talent that he's got."

It is this instinctive nature of his acting that protects him from being overshadowed. British TV is a veritable playfield of giants of comedy and Atkinson has shared screen with most of them. Veterans like Stephen Fry and Hugh Laurie have the potential of eating up any artist simply by deploying their well timed histrionics. However, with Atkinson, their monumental talent only enhances the canvass already created by the understated hyper comedy.   Black Adder was Rowan Atkinson all the way despite the presence of stalwarts with scene grabbing lines.   This happens because he is not dependent on props to create humour. He is great in wordy comedies like Black Adder and equally devastating in the physical laugh riot of Mr Bean.

His knack of zeroing in on the vitals of his character and chiselling away the distraction till only the core remains is the very definition of acting itself. After distillation what remains is unadulterated and super-refined comedy.

Dr House- Sherlock Holmes as Diagnostician

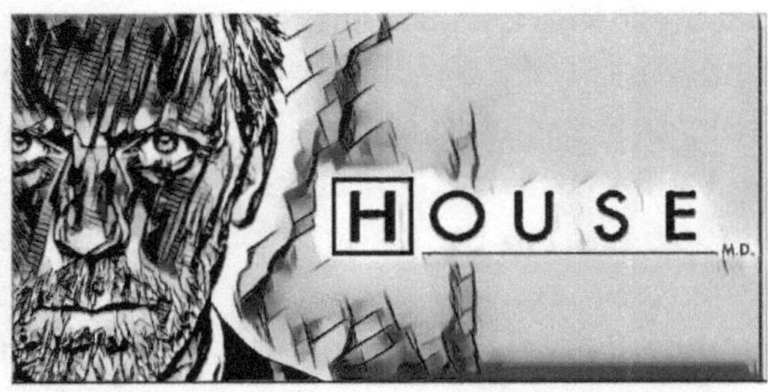

One needs to watch Black Adder or Jeeves and Wooster to appreciate the work that Hugh Laurie put in his very successful TV series House, M.D. He is an epitome of British buffoonery and does the wide eyed impersonation of an unadulterated moron with aplomb. Here, in his American transition he is speaking American with gusto and relishing the role of an acerbic, drug addict, low on etiquette diagnostician of supernatural abilities. One of the hilarious videos on YouTube depicts him taking a quiz on American slang and failing miserably. Completely non British environs of Princeton-Plainsboro Teaching Hospital may look alien for Wooster but roots of the character are patently British- Sherlock Holmes.

Arthur Conan Doyle has created an immortal character. More than that, he has created a framework of a character where his despicable social skills are condoned only due to his first rate intellect. In fact, the ability to zero in to the crux of the situation is the key reason for most of his bad behavior. Niceties are not for Holmes who cuts the crap a bit too fast for comfort. His method is based on deduction and he is given to substance abuse and plays musical instruments with some dexterity. Hugh Laurie identifies with the essential Britishness of his character that is uncannily modeled on Holmes. Dr Gregory House is socially maladjusted, addicted to painkillers and abhors comfort as an obstacle in the way of his deductions. Mystery in his case is about the diagnosis. He is an accomplished pianist and guitarist. He is not into people and avoids contact with patients and deals mainly with his mystery. He puts his mental capability above all comforts and happiness.

Such qualities get accentuated with his racist and misogynistic remarks which come with impeccable logic but with total disregard for good taste. This relentless barrage needs interpreters that keep on reminding the readers/viewers that the genius is following the right moral direction. This task was given to Watson in Conan Doyle's world. Here we have Wilson, played with exceptional empathy by Robert Sean Leonard. Playing the role of interpreter, springboard of ideas and a perpetual punching bag by a man of exceptional caliber is critical to the genre created by Holmes. The series self-consciously conforms to the genre. Tributes come in the form of trivia, some subtle, some obvious. House is a play on Holmes/Homes. Watson becomes Wilson. Even the flat number is 221-B.

Hugh Laurie's main achievement is making the character appealing in spite of his despicable qualities. Laurie achieves traction with his impeccable timing for sarcasm and grudging admiration without ever verbalizing it. He channelizes wit, vulnerability and brilliance through his character which is a difficult conductor of such exalted virtues. Characters of this breed require a degree of magnetism and Laurie brings that charm with him without being too obvious about it. He tunes in to the mischievous elements of his character with great felicity. His torments are made palatable on screen by the sheer deliciousness with which he delivers them. This is not to undermine the support he gets from the cast. We interpret him through their reaction to him. If they are suitably impressed, so are we. That said, Laurie brings a lot of nuances and undercurrent with his acting depth. To quote a review from Slant magazine "the show rests heavily on Laurie's shoulders and his ability to recite his lines with a delicate, if sure-minded, punch. The UK native has the chops to hold the hour-long show together despite its drawbacks."

YES PRIME MINSTER: COMEDY AS IT SHOULD BE

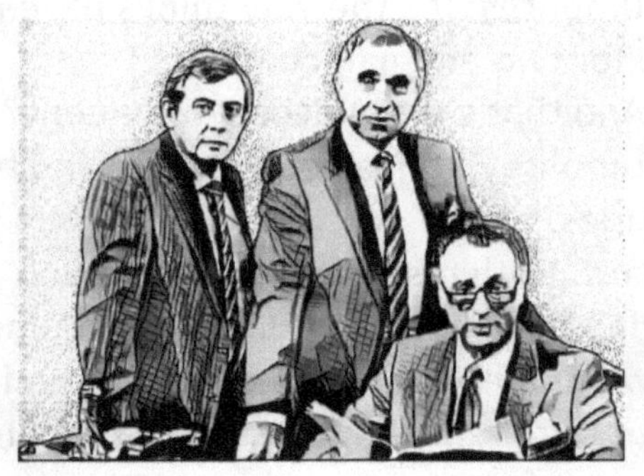

'Yes Prime Minister' was first aired almost 40 years ago after three hilarious seasons of 'Yes Minister' and the unexpected rise of Jim Hacker to the Prime Ministership. Both the series depict the sweet irony of administration and governance where common sense has no role in the labyrinth of procedure and rules.

In the 'Grand Design' the inaugural episode of iconic British Comedy the conversation between the lead characters the newly elevated Prime Minister Rt Honerable Jim Hacker, his Cabinet Secretary Sir Humphrey and His Principal Private Secretary Bernard goes like this.

Jim: So we haven't got somebody here to cater for me.

Sir Humphrey: It's the way things have been done for two and half centuries.

Jim: And that's the clinching argument?

Sir Humphrey: It has been for two and half centuries.

Bernard: With respect Sir Humphrey, it couldn't have been the clinching argument for two and half centuries, because half a century ago it had only been the clinching argument for two centuries, and a century ago it had only been the clinching argument for one and half centuries.

Those who have seen the series must be smiling at the memory of the faces of the dramatis personae. This delicious repartee is just one example of alchemy of superb comic timing, crisp script and top notch acting that created the enduring appeal of the legendary sitcom. The series has run all over the world and had many local adaptations. In Hindi we had particularly successful 'Jee mantraji' and 'Ji Pradhan Mantriji'. Farookh Sheikh and Jayant Kriplani were great. Manohar Shyam Joshi's 'Netaji Kahin' was another masterpiece from the genre. The original twin series from the BBC stable are timeless classics.

Stalling has been raised to the level of art. Hacker, played by Paul Eddington, is a politician, self-serving with all the flaws of his tribe (blatant corruption was sidestepped). At the same time he wants to leave a legacy and do something good for the people. What he had not bargained for was Humphrey Appleby, "unflappable symbol of a machine that has no gears, only brakes." Utterly snobbish and elitist Sir Humphrey (Nigel Hawthorne) is a quintessential parody of a bureaucrat with an almost frightening resonance of realism. Bernard (Derek Fowlds) is Private Secretary of the Minister he is into puns and intricacies of the language. His deadpan interjections are some of the most uproarious moments of this great series. In 'The Tangled Web' the issue is phone-tapping and Jim is uncomfortable about it. Ultimately he too sees the virtues of it when he is told that he too is in the 'death list' but not before some side-splitting exchanges sample this.

Jim: Anyway, why are we bugging Hugh Halifax, is he talking to the Russians?
Sir Humphrey: No, the French actually, that's much more serious.
Jim: Why?
Bernard: Well the Russians already know what we're doing.

Irreverence is a much desired ingredient of comedy. It is achieved by not being bothered by the holy cows and finding a fresh take on conventions. However, being frantic about conveying irreverence may simply bury the comedy. Yes Minister and later Yes Prime Minister hit the sweet spot where irreverence meets with the light touch of superb timing to create timeless magic. It is all the more credible as it was achieved in the field of Politics. Ironically, a goldmine of comic situations, politics has been more successfully exploited by other genres such as crime, intrigue or thrillers. The twin series are the crowning achievement of British situation comedy- an unbelievably rich field of accomplishments.

Political comedy is found to be difficult and has a tendency to degenerate into lampooning. The twin series were authentic.

Nothing may have happened actually but nothing was beyond the pale of actually happening. Nothing was sacrosanct but everything was somehow believable. Once again from 'Man Overboard' Jim asks about the figures given to him "and all this is absolutely honest and accurate?" To which Sir Humphrey replies "It comes from the Ministry of Defence" to which Jim says "even though it could be honest and accurate". Irreverence is coming from comedy not the other way round.

We in India, baptised in the Westminster Model of parliamentary democracy, have much to identify with in the series. The series depends on the clash between Civil Service and politicians. They have very different moral codes and objectives, both of which have to project an image of unity, harmony and common purpose. Co-Writer Anthony Jay said later "what comedy writer could ask for more? And yet there is more. Both the minister and the permanent secretary are committed to maintaining the pretence that the minister is the expert, all-powerful boss, and the permanent secretary is the docile servant, obediently awaiting instructions. The reality, of course, is the exact opposite....It is the servant-wiser-than-master joke, so successfully exploited in Jeeves and The Admirable Crichton." Our own Akbar-Birbal can also be fitted in this category. Not that the master does not know the reality. The more you know, funnier it gets. Jim says in one of the episodes "the three articles of Civil Service faith: it takes longer to do things quickly, it's more expensive to do them cheaply and it's more democratic to do them in secret". Yes Minister and Yes Prime Minister made this hilarity blindingly obvious to people across cultures.

Margret Thatcher was a fan. In fact she went on to script a small episode for the series with lead actors taking part. It was not a big success but indicates the cult following it enjoyed and still does. Issues like open government, University spending, environment, privacy, youth rebelliousness and austerity continue to pose enough challenges to governance. It is still providing fodder to the comedy empire consisting of cartoons, late night shows and stand up comedy. Campus protests, Wikileaks and fee riots in Britain have exposed us to situations whose comic perspective was so vividly given to us by Hacker, Humphrey and Bernard. Anthony Jay further said "Jonathan (Co-author) and I are sometimes described as satirists, but that is not how we see ourselves. Satirists are trying to change things; we are happy just to enjoy the comic possibilities of things as they are and share the discovery with our fellow citizens."

While Bernard is afflicted with 'fondness for awful puns and maddening pedantry', Sir Humphrey's Machiavellian skills are' often accompanied by brain-wrenching sentences designed to confuse Hacker - and often succeeding.' This is a sample from one rare instance (from- The Skeleton in the Cupboard) where tables are turned and Sir Humphrey is at the receiving end.

Sir Humphrey: Minister I think there is something that perhaps you ought to know.
Jim: Yes Humphrey.
Sir Humphrey: The identity of the official whose alleged responsibility for this hypothetical oversight has been the subject of recent discussion, is, not shrouded in quite such impenetrable obscurity as certain previous disclosures may have led you to assume, but not to put too fine a point on it,

the individual in question is, it may surprise you to learn, one whose present interlocutor, is in the habit of defining by means of the perpendicular pronoun.
Jim: Beg your pardon.
Sir Humphrey: It was I.

As opposed to this is Bernard at his pedantic best in 'The Bed of Nails'-

Jim: But if I pull it off then it would be a feather in my cap.
Bernard: If you pull it off Minister it won't be in your cap any more.

By highlighting the comic possibilities of everyday politics and governance BBC has created a classic in the true sense of the word. It has not dated and it has straddled the boundaries of diverse cultures. It is perpetually on air in some or the other network all over the world. A theatre version opened this year to critical acclaim in England. Diverse countries like India, Ukraine and Holland have created their local versions. It has been translated in various languages. A virtual piracy empire has been created around it on the Internet and DVDs. A superbly executed piece of art, the twin series captures the gentle hypocrisy of politics and bureaucracy with an unfailing grasp on the humour of it all. Therein lies its appeal.

V S Naipaul: Raw Nerves in a Free State

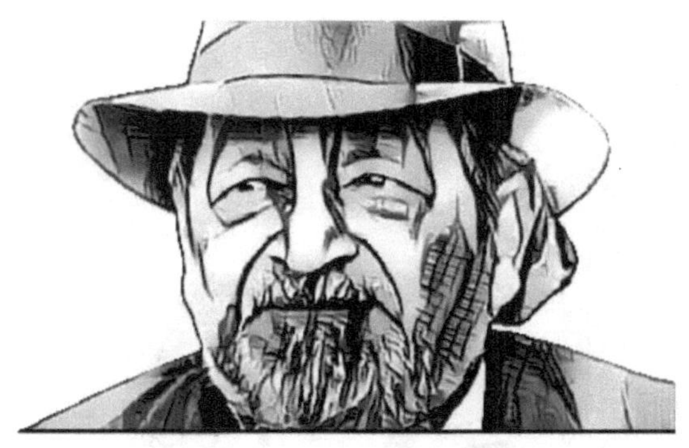

His 'raw nerves' have been a calling card for V S Naipaul throughout his long creative career. He made an art form out of being prickly. This nerviness helped him to come to terms with being a man with no past. He was always conscious of being a double exile (Indian from Trinidad writing in England). Initially, he just had a settled ambition to become a writer without knowing how to go about it. There was always a nagging feeling in him that he does not have the rich background of a civilizational past and established literary pointers or landmarks that are available to 'metropolitan' writers of Europe and from other rich ancient traditions. His past, as Trinidadian Indian, ended at his grandfather - an indentured labour. He started with personal memories and created masterpiece like 'A House for Mr. Biswas' but he realized that a genuine exploration of his writerly ambition will not be fully realized if he does not find a way to transcend deficiencies of his limited background. His remarkable life and distinguished literary career is a saga of getting enriched by tackling a deficient base and finding new ways of being a literary chronicler of one's time. His 'raw nerves' were a handy tool in this enterprise, never letting him settle in views and giving him a formidable reputation as "Cantankerous Curmudgeon".

A Miraculous Ambition

V S Naipaul rightly credits his father Seepersad Naipaul to give him an ambition to write. The senior Naipaul, who was son of an indentured labour — a class just a handshake short of slaves, quite remarkably, found resourcefulness to educate himself enough to be a lover of literature and become a journalist. He also realized his ambition to be a writer though in a very limited way. V S Naipaul openly admits that he internalized the ambition to be a writer even before he knew what being a writer entails.

Naipaul has extensively and famously examined his writing impulse on many occasions. He wrote "I write the artificial, self-conscious beginnings of many books; until finally some true impulse—the one I have been working toward—possesses me, and I sail away on my year's labor. And that is mysterious still—that out of artifice one should touch and stir up what is deepest in one's soul, one's heart, one's memory." This great mysterious stepping-stone of literature of reaching the most genuine, deepest and real through the artifice helped him in the beginning. He is on record about sitting in the Freelance Room of BBC World Service building – an old hotel, and started populating the characters of his lived-in street of his childhood Port of Spain. It flew and helped him write his initial books. He became the poet of communities with short memory pools and half-baked societies.

His is a story of sheer ambition. He willed himself into being a writer. His apprenticeship with his father and scholarship to Oxford bear testimony to the power of a nurturing environment. This is also an ode to the power of literature. V S and his father developed this burning desire to be writer just by the exposure to quality work of Shakespeare, Huxley, O Henry etc. without having any literary ecosystem of history, community, context or resources. He stayed with his ambition, testing its ability to tell his realities. He was helped by an unsparing eye, absence of melodrama and above all boundless talent.

Seepersad, who died in his forties when Naipaul was at Oxford with a scholarship, succeeded through his son, who almost closed the loop by becoming one of the most accomplished masters of English prose and being the most prominent literary voice of the last century. The Nobel Prize was just sealing the obvious.

Limits of literary forms

A surging Naipaul mastered novels. His 'A House for Mr. Biswas', 'A Bend in the River' and 'Enigma of Arrival' are out there with prime examples of novel as a literary form.

His voice is deep, comical and authentic. His technique impeccable and his imagination rich. But his 'raw nerves' were at play once again. He was getting impatient with the limitations of novel form to tell the story of his time. In his own words.

"For sixty or seventy years in the nineteenth century the novel in Europe, developing very fast in the hands of a relay of masters, became an extraordinary tool. It did what no other literary form—essay, poem, drama, history—could do. It gave industrial or industrialising or modern society a very clear idea of itself. It showed with immediacy what hadn't been shown before; and it altered vision. Certain things in the form could be modified or played with later, but the pattern of the modern novel had been set, and its programme laid out. All of us who have come after have been derivative. We can never be the first again. We might bring new material from far away, but the programme we are following has been laid out for us."

His sense of not having the historical richness of a 'metropolitan' writer is also at work here. That and his prickly raw nerves.

He can't withstand the feeling of being derivative. He wrote "What is good is what is new, in both form and content". He, who entered the authentic and deep through artifice, was very clear that "what is good forgets whatever models it might have had and is unexpected; we have to catch it on the wing.   Writing of this quality cannot be taught in a writing course".

Naipaul, ever prickly with staleness, was looking for new ways of expressing himself. He lamented "Late twentieth century needs another kind of interpretation. But the novel, still (in spite of appearances) mimicking the programme of nineteenth century originators, still feeding off the vision they created can subtly distort the unaccommodating new reality". With this he moves in for kill as he is an explorer not a prophet. Ever evolving, ever processing, with no tolerance for stale, inauthentic or derivative.   In   his   characteristic contemptuous way he damns novel:-

"As a form it is now commonplace enough, and limited enough to be teachable. ….. It is a vanity of the age (and commercial promotion) that the novel continues to be literature's final and highest expression". This realization led him to embark on what, very insufficiently, referred to as his travel writings. His non-fiction repertoire is as large as his fiction and is responsible for much of his acerbic literary persona.

As he agitated against mimicry of 19th century programme by 20th century novel, he was equally aghast by the newly independent societies ineptly 'mimicking' the societies of their former masters and losing their 'wholeness'. He is "oddly romantic" about the 'wholeness' of culture in Africa that lurks beneath the shallow upper layer of mimicry. Ian Buruma, who has anointed Naipaul as 'poet of the displaced', has very perceptively explored the connection between his raw nerve and obsession with wholeness and totally ruthless intolerance for phoniness of mimicry. He was unsparing about these newly freed societies – he called India a 'greater hurt' and his first visit ended "in futility and impatience a gratuitous act of cruelty, self reproach and flight". His 'raw nerves' never created enough bile for him to become 'an apologist of the empire'. Colonial plunder led to wiping out of these cultures and leaving "half-baked, dispossessed, rootless societies" losing their "wholeness". He is clear-eyed about the deficiencies of these societies. Summing up the connect between his raw nerves, wholeness and mimicky, Buruma writes

"He understood people who were culturally dislocated and who tried to find solace in religious or political fantasies that were often borrowed from other places and ineptly mimicked. He described such delusions precisely and often comically. His sense of humor sometimes bordered on cruelty, and in interviews with liberal journalists it could take the form of calculated provocation. But his refusal to sentimentalize the wounds in postcolonial societies produced some of his most penetrating insights."

The Believer

His acerbic wit, his 'calculated provocations' gained him a well deserved reputation of an ill-tempered intellectual. He provokes and is masterfully disdainful in his put-downs. He is provocative about pseudo romanticization of tribal societies. He is often compared to Conrad in this regard, though he, with his characteristic lack of modesty, finds 'A bend in the River', 'much much better than Conrad'. He might have a point there. While Conrad appears settled in his bleak and settled view of the 'bush' the 'darkness'. He was occupying a pulpit from where he was pontificating. Whereas, Naipaul, with all his sweeping contempt for the darkness, appears to be an explorer in action rather than a prophet with his unchanging edicts.

He is always aware that he can revisit the enigma of these societies. In fact, India was revisited so was his most controversial works on Islamic countries. In India, he saw signs of redemption in his later books but he remained steadfast in the issues with Islam. He was so caustic in writing on Islam that his Nobel, in the immediate aftermath of the 9/11 terrorism attack on WTC, New York, was seen as political. But it was lauded by many. Philip Hensher was quoted in a 2002 Atlantic article "If ever there was a moment when external considerations might have discouraged the Nobel committee from rewarding the author of Among the Believers, that magnificently disdainful journey through Islam, this is it." Despite this, he has been accused of being

Islamophobe by Edward Said. Derek Walcott called him a racist. He has been accused of aping bigoted ways of colonialists. His statements have been found openly offensive in LGBT circles. He damned Forster and Keynes with clear hatred dripping with withering sarcasm for their homosexuality. His views on Islam have been derided and also celebrated for his 'terrifying honesty'.

All said and done, Sir V S Naipaul was a deeply unpleasant man to us mortals. He was cruel, sadomasochist (his treatment of his wife, mistress and boast of being a 'great prostitute man' are cases in point) , a penny-pincher and a snob. No doubt, but what he was not was - a mimic. His unpleasantness was rooted in his 'terrifying honesty'. He was clear when a mistress had served her purpose, place of his wife in his life, entry of his second wife into his home the very next day when his long suffering first wife was laid to rest after a long cancer battle. His famous one liners verging on sadistic, racist and heartless always originated from his core clarity, which was both his bane and strength. He was always authentic - that does not mean that we have to like his nastiness. A life dedicated to refining perception and constant honing of touchstone of self can result in a terribly clear and chiselled beacon, which guides and terrifies in equal measure.

Milan Kundera Remains a Pleasure to Read

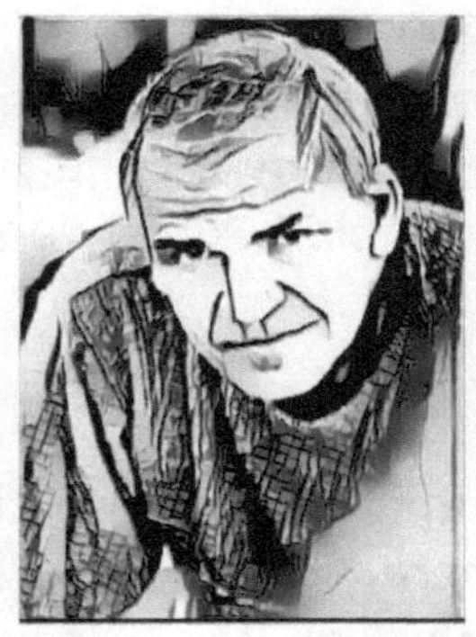

Milan Kundera was a writer of moments, of fleeting experiences or even further sub division or an interpretation of that emotion. He likes to call his method or style as 'meditative interrogation' or 'interrogative meditation'. However, those delightfully ponderous and long meditation are almost always about a moment as said above, a fleeting one. It can be about an old lady waving goodbye or a rather disgruntled look at the female midriff. Fleeting or momentary this might be but Kundera weaves lifetimes out of it.

Old masters, here I am talking in terms of age, tend to acquire a telegraphic leanness in their output. In case of writing, often, paragraphs start looking something like formulae- Condensed and distilled – expressing core truth with the benefit of commentary. This can go either way. It might strike as a whiplash of understanding or leave the trail of unsatisfied craving for understanding sometimes.

Autumnal output by master authors swings in one more direction. The author sleepwalks through the product. Due to innate greatness or 'muscular memory', broad parameters of the products are usually in place and it has some signature flashes of genius. But this work fades in comparison to earlier works which were less of products of practice but of genuine inspiration supported by indefatigable craftsmanship. Soul simply does not shine through. Admirers of the artist get into nostalgia mode and start celebrating diminished sparks that remind them of the original fire – their own and that of the artist. But, as I mentioned somewhere else, nostalgia has both its utility and futility. 'Festival of insignificance' Milan Kundera's only novel in this millennium, a 115 page telegraph of a novel, exemplifies all the facets of aging maestros discussed above. But, a fan, like yours truly can't but be thrilled by the offering.

'Festival of Insignificance' is a sparse stark reminder of Kundera's core capability of analysing a moment/feeling/situation/concept and seeing how that can pervade the much larger canvas of life despite seemingly niche quality. Kundera has great powers of perception to grasp the underlying ingredient of a situation and deploys his meditative interrogation with great success. Here, he dwells on insignificance as the leitmotif of human existence and has developed an enjoyable book. The novel, despite its sparse bulk, is able to cater to the ruminative cravings of the reader. However, one can't shake the feeling that Kundera is playing like a retired or retiring player. He has retained his key capabilities but the novel needs more. However, the fact remains that the Master always delivers, at least to the basic minimum level, even when he is sleepwalking.

It has given rise to voices in many quarters doubting the continued significance of Milan Kundera. In an article titled 'How important is Milan Kundera today? in the Guardian Jonathan Coe writes "The Festival of Insignificance, then, is certainly typical Kundera, if not classic Kundera. It is an old man's book and, while there are flickering signs of a mellow and playful wisdom, it would be surprising if there were not something autumnal about it. A glance at the back covers of Kundera's novels in the Faber editions reveals a raft of quotes from the likes of Ian McEwan, Salman Rushdie and Carlos Fuentes, most of them more than 30 years old, reminding us that his reputation was at its zenith in the 1980s, the decade when everybody was reading The Book of Laughter and Forgetting and The Unbearable Lightness of Being." Another article in Atlantic Monthly 'Does Milan Kundera Still Matter?' says "Reading Kundera in the '80s was like watching Mad Men with the conviction that smoking, drinking, and grabbing the secretary's ass were bold assertions of individual autonomy in the face of a cruelly repressive state.

Czech Communism collapsed 25 years ago. Kundera, who is 86, has lived in France for 40 years and written in French for more than two decades. The Festival of Insignificance—his first novel in 13 years—is an excellent opportunity to ask what happens to his fiction once the backdrop of Soviet oppression no longer throws his dark jokes, nihilism, and naughty interludes into bright relief."

Such observation may be valid and writing in Kundera style may no longer be having its novelty kick but that does not take away much from his importance. He is a great novelist and a pioneer for his style which he himself confesses is in the tradition of great European novelists. His key works stand the test of time and resonate with brilliance that appeals to human concerns beyond certain epochs. His best works contain the intellectual and emotional pleasure of an examined life. His capabilities of "forging connections between the individual consciousness and the shifting currents of history and politics" has the thrum of operatic proportion and never fails to elate. This sophistication of feelings which hovers in the no man's land of psycho-philosophical fiction.

He has mastered the art of deploying the tool of novelistic inquiry to issues of his choosing and that has often led to a hugely satisfactory literary pay off. His key works of the so-called middle period are the foundation of his reputation. The Book of Laughter and Forgetting, The Unbearable Lightness of Being and Immortality will find place in any pantheon of great novels for the intensity of their inquiry, their amusement at the complication that grim realities of life throw at us. Despite their playfulness, irony and ponderous meditation these novels were and remain urgent due to their evident connection with the zeitgeist.

One of the qualities of great literature is that its esoteric highbrow abstraction does not affect its accessibility. Kundera's seemingly obtuse phenomenological (a term that he politely refuses) inquiries are illuminated with the easy recognition. Reader never feels distant from the text despite 'interiority' of the material.

Kundera has achieved a unique voice in his books. A playful wisdom that abhors seriousness. He may look formidable due to his erudition and European sensibilities but he is never serious. The twinkling naughtiness of his voice, that impish tone is sure shot antidote to dogma. This is also a protective armour that saves the scepticism from being fossilised into dogma of his own. With these voices he confidently 'pursues the lost possibilities'.

This pursuit is essentially interrogative. Frequency of questions in his text is only overtaken by the open refusal to subscribe unambiguously to any point or belief. Even the most extensive enquiries yield answers that have an air of work-in-progress. This is not tentativeness on his part, simply an acknowledgement of the logic of evolution that human issues don't lend themselves to final answers.

Much of requiem for Kundera's relevance centres around the fact that his strengths like taste for irony, philosophical gravitas, essayistic style has been either equalled or overtaken by later writers like Julian Barnes and Alain de Botton to Slavoj Žižek. This should be seen as another instance of his greatness if he is able to inspire greatness. As an original he retains his primacy. If he discovered a genre or a style that is still relevant enough to attract great talent, credit is all his.